lyrics by

Sting

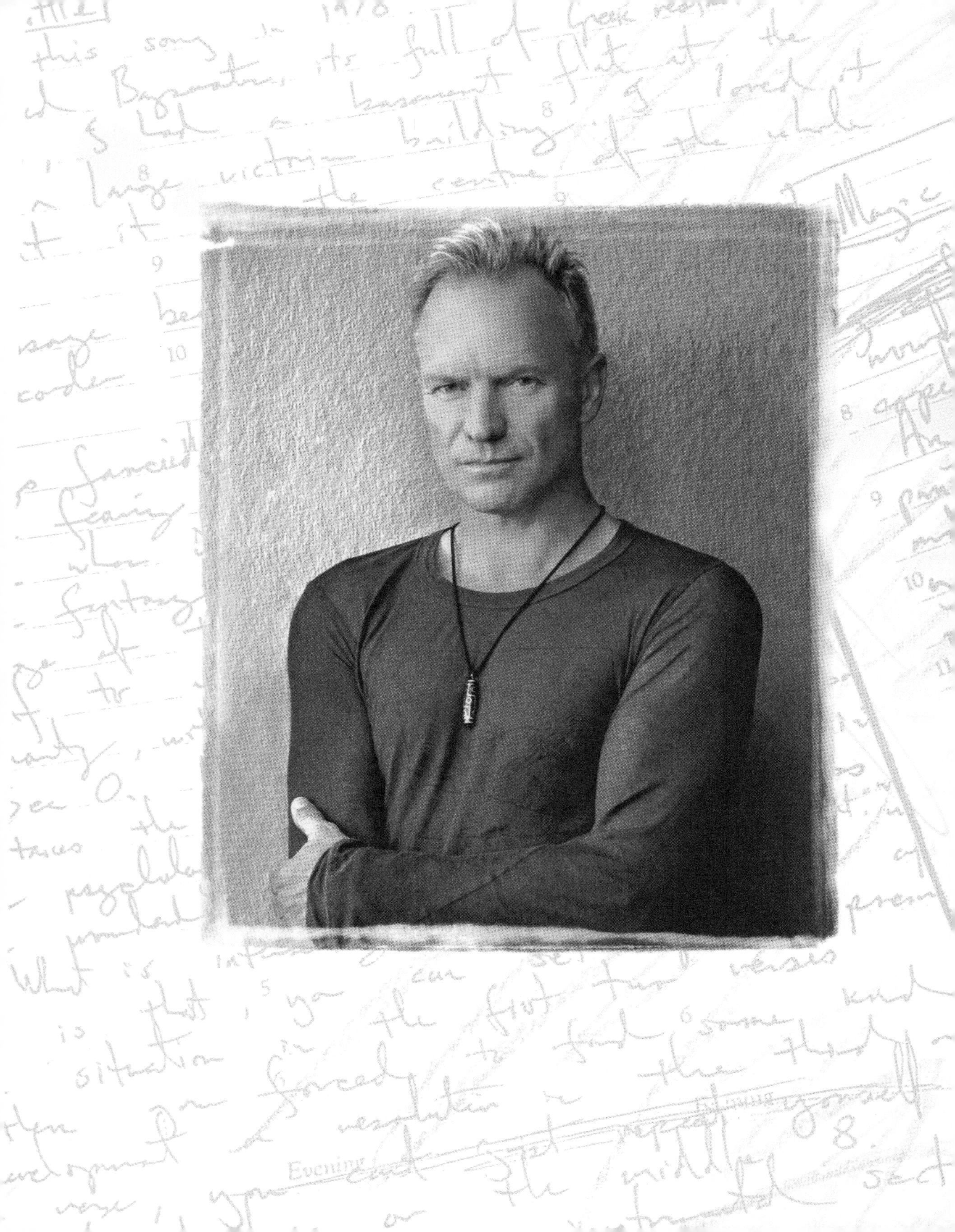

lyrics by

Sting

the dial press

THE DIAL PRESS

LYRICS
A Dial Press Book / October 2007

Published by The Dial Press
A Division of Random House, Inc.
New York, New York

Book design by Virginia Norey

The Dial Press is a registered trademark of Random House, Inc.,
and the colophon is a trademark of Random House, Inc.

Library of Congress Cataloging-in-Publication Data

Sting (Musician)
[Songs. Selections. Texts]
Lyrics / by Sting.
p. cm.
ISBN-13: 978-0-385-33987-2 (hardcover)
1. Songs--Texts. 2. Sting (Musician) I. Title.
ML54.6.S85S66 2007
782.42166'0268--dc22
2007030296

Printed in the United States of America
Published simultaneously in Canada

www.dialpress.com

RRC 10 9 8 7 6 5 4 3 2 1

Contents

Publishing my lyrics separately from their musical accompaniment is something that I've studiously avoided until now. The two, lyrics and music, have always been mutually dependent, in much the same way as a mannequin and a set of clothes are dependent on each other; separate them, and what remains is a naked dummy and a pile of cloth. Nevertheless, the exercise has been an interesting one, seeing perhaps for the first time how successfully the lyrics survive on their own, and inviting the question as to whether song lyrics are in fact poetry or something else entirely. And while I've never seriously described myself as a poet, the book in your hands, devoid as it is of any musical notation, looks suspiciously like a book of poems.

So it seems I am entering, with some trepidation, the unadorned realm of the poet. I have set out my compositions in the sequence they were written and provided a little background when I thought it might be illuminating. My wares have neither been sorted nor dressed in clothes that do not belong to them; indeed, they have been shorn of the very garments that gave them their shape in the first place. No doubt some of them will perish in the cold cruelty of this new environment, and yet others may prove more resilient and become perhaps more beautiful in their naked state. I can't predict the outcome, but I have taken this risk knowingly and, while no one in their right mind should ever attempt to set "The Waste Land" to music, in the hopeful words of T. S. Eliot, These fragments I have shored against my ruins.

Next to You

So Lonely

Roxanne

Hole in My Life

Peanuts

Can't Stand Losing You

Truth Hits Everybody

Born in the '50s

◆

Visions of the Night

Our first album as the Police was recorded piecemeal
in a run-down studio above a dairy in Leatherhead. We had
been together as a band for roughly a year by then. Some of the
songs had been written for my previous band, Last Exit, and
adapted for the new one. Others had been composed while
touring, and some were created during rehearsals or
while recording.

We weren't signed to a record company yet, and none of us
had any money, so we used some secondhand tapes that we
found in our manager's garage and recorded very late at night,
for an even cheaper studio rate: moonlighting only after
another band had left.

We'd work until the coffee ran out and we were bleary-eyed
and delirious with exhaustion and the absurdity of our
arguments.

I'd drive back to London in my battered old Citroën in a kind of euphoria, with these tunes thundering in my head, yelling improvised lyrics at the top of my voice to the empty road and the stars twinkling sceptically above the rooftops.

I'd get back to my flat in Bayswater just as the sun was coming up through the trees in Hyde Park, thinking that these were some of the best days and weeks of my life. I'd try to scribble down whatever I'd been declaiming in the car and then go to sleep for the rest of the morning.

The afternoon would be spent trying to make sense of these fragments and working on them until early evening so that I would have something presentable that night.

I was happy because I'd dreamed about this, this making of an album, for as long as I'd owned a guitar, strummed my first chord, and rhymed my first couplet. It was almost too much to absorb.

There's no grand concept at work in this album, just a loose collection of dreams, fragments and fantasies, low doggerel and high dudgeon, sense and nonsense, anger and romance, all welded together by the bluff and bluster of a new band.

We were insane in our optimism, and we were never happier.

Next to You

I can't stand it for another day
When you live so many miles away
Nothing here is gonna make me stay
You took me over, let me find a way

I sold my house
I sold my motor, too
All I want is to be next to you
I'd rob a bank
Maybe steal a plane
You took me over
Think I'm goin' insane

What can I do
All I want is to be next to you
What can I do
All I want is to be next to you

I've had a thousand girls or maybe more
But I've never felt like this before
But I just don't know what's come over me
You took me over, take a look at me

What can I do
All I want is to be next to you
What can I do
All I want is to be next to you

All I want is to be next to you
All I want is to be next to you
All I want is to be next to you

So many times I used to give a sign
Got this feeling, gonna lose my mind
When all it is is just a love affair
You took me over, baby, take me there

What can I do
All I want is to be next to you
What can I do
All I want is to be next to you
What can I do
All I want is to be next to you
What can I do
All I want is to be next to you

All I want is to be next to you . . .

I wrote these lyrics while I was in Last Exit and then grafted them shamelessly onto the chords from Bob Marley's "No Woman, No Cry." This kind of musical juxtaposition—the lilting rhythm of the verses separated by monolithic slabs of straight rock and roll—pleased the hell out of me. That we could achieve it effortlessly just added to the irony of a song about misery being sung so joyously.

It was something of a coup when someone pointed out to BBC television that, because of my poor diction, I seemed to be singing the name of a popular TV presenter, Sue Lawley, and not "So lonely." It was played on national television as an homage to Sue, but we didn't complain. Blessings are often unexpected.

So Lonely

Well someone told me yesterday
That when you throw your love away
You act as if you don't care
You look as if you're going somewhere

But I just can't convince myself
I couldn't live with no one else
And I can only play that part
And sit and nurse my broken heart

So lonely
So lonely
So lonely
So lonely

So lonely
So lonely
So lonely
So lonely . . .

Now no one's knocked upon my door
For a thousand years or more

All made up and nowhere to go
Welcome to this one-man show

Just take a seat they're always free
No surprise no mystery
In this theatre that I call my soul
I always play the starring role

So lonely
So lonely
So lonely
So lonely

So lonely
So lonely
So lonely
So lonely . . .

A friend of mine bought a sheet of lyrics for "Roxanne" *that had turned up in a collection of memorabilia, and he asked me to verify if it was genuine.*

"Well, that's my handwriting," I said, "and those are my doodles": three clocks—one at five to four, another at ten past six, and one sidelong that looks to be showing eight o'clock—a sundial, an hourglass, five sets of five-bar gates that prisoners use to mark the passing of the days, some kind of whirlwind vortex spinning in the top right-hand corner, and a spear or an arrowhead. I imagine I was drawing these as I was listening back to various takes of the vocals, but I don't know what they mean.

I wrote "Roxanne" in Paris in 1977. The band was staying in a seedy hotel near the Gare St.-Lazare. I had a set of descending chords starting in G minor and a melancholy frame of mind. Inspired by the romance and sadness of Edmond Rostand's great play Cyrano de Bergerac *and the prostitutes on the street below my window, "Roxanne" came to life.*

I've sung this song on most of the nights of my life since then, and it's my job to sing it with the same freshness and enthusiasm as if I'd written it that afternoon and not thirty years previously. I always manage to find something new in it and I'm still grateful.

Roxanne

Roxanne
You don't have to put on the red light
Those days are over
You don't have to sell your body to the night

Roxanne
You don't have to wear that dress tonight
Walk the streets for money
You don't care if it's wrong or if it's right

Roxanne
You don't have to put on the red light
Roxanne
You don't have to put on the red light

Roxanne (Put on the red light)
Roxanne (Put on the red light)
Roxanne (Put on the red light)
Roxanne (Put on the red light)
Roxanne (Put on the red light)
Roxanne

I loved you since I knew you
I wouldn't talk down to you
I have you to tell just how I feel
I won't share you with another boy

I know my mind is made up
So put away your makeup
Told you once I won't tell you again
It's a bad way

Roxanne
You don't have to put on the red light
Roxanne
You don't have to put on the red light

Roxanne (Put on the red light)
Roxanne (Put on the red light)
Roxanne (Put on the red light)

Hole in My Life

There's a hole
In my life
There's a hole
In my life

Shadow in my heart
Is tearing me apart
Or maybe it's just something
In my stars

There's a hole
In my life
There's a hole
In my life

Be a happy man
I try the best I can
Or maybe I'm just looking
For too much

There's something missing from my life
Cuts me open like a knife
It leaves me vulnerable
I have this disease
I shake like an incurable
God help me please

Oh, there's a hole
In my life
There's a hole
In my life

I'd been asked to contribute some lyrics for this tune by *Stewart Copeland—it was one of those I composed in the car on the way home from Leatherhead. I was thinking about a former musical hero who had dwindled to a mere celebrity, and I was more than willing to pass judgment on his extracurricular activities in the tabloids, never thinking for a moment that I would suffer the same distorted perceptions at their hands a few years later.*

Peanuts

It's all a game
You're not the same
Your famous name
The price of fame

Oh no
Try to liberate me
I said oh no
Stay and irritate me
I said oh no
Try to elevate me
I said oh no
Just a fallen hero

Don't wanna hear about the drugs you're taking
Don't wanna read about the love you're making
Don't wanna hear about the life you're faking
Don't wanna read about the muck they're raking

You sang your song
For much too long
The songs they're wrong
The bread has gone

Oh no
Try to liberate me

I said oh no
Stay and irritate me
I said oh no
Try to elevate me
I said oh no
Just a fallen hero

Don't wanna hear about the drugs you're taking
Don't wanna read about the love you're making
Don't wanna hear about the life you're faking
Don't wanna read about the muck they're raking

It's all a game
You're not the same
Your famous name
The price of fame

Oh no
Try to liberate me
I said oh no
Stay and irritate me
I said oh no
Try to elevate me
I said oh no
Just a fallen hero
Oh, you're just a fallen hero

Don't wanna hear about the drugs you're taking
Don't wanna read about the love you're making
Don't wanna hear about the life you're faking
Don't wanna read about the muck they're raking

Don't wanna find out what you've been taking
Don't wanna read about the love you're making
Don't wanna hear about the life you're faking
Don't wanna read about the muck they're raking

Don't wanna find out what you've been taking
Don't wanna read about the love you're making
Don't wanna hear about the life you're faking
Don't wanna read about the muck they're raking

Peanuts, peanuts
Peanuts

Oh, no, no
Oh, no, no
Oh, no, no
Oh, no, no
Oh, no, no
Oh

Can't Stand Losing You

I've called you so many times today
And I guess it's all true what your girlfriends say
That you don't ever want to see me again
And your brother's gonna kill me and he's six feet ten
I guess you'd call it cowardice
But I'm not prepared to go on like this

I can't, I can't
I can't stand losing
I can't, I can't
I can't stand losing
I can't, I can't
I can't
I can't stand losing you
I can't stand losing you
I can't stand losing you
I can't stand losing you

I see you've sent my letters back
And my LP records and they're all scratched
I can't see the point in another day
When nobody listens to a word I say
You can call it lack of confidence
But to carry on living doesn't make no sense
I can't, I can't
I can't stand losing
I can't, I can't
I can't stand losing
I can't, I can't
I can't stand losing
I can't, I can't
I can't stand losing . . .

I guess this is our last good-bye
And you don't care so I won't cry
But you'll be sorry when I'm dead

And all this guilt will be on your head
I guess you'd call it suicide
But I'm too full to swallow my pride

I can't, I can't
I can't stand losing . . .

I can't stand losing you

Truth Hits Everybody

Sleep lay behind me like a broken ocean
Strange waking dreams before my eyes unfold
You lay there sleeping like an open doorway
I stepped outside myself and felt so cold

Take a look at my new toy
It'll blow your head in two, oh boy

Truth hits everybody
Truth hits everyone
Oh, oh, oh
Truth hits everybody
Truth hits everyone
Truth hits everybody
Truth hits everyone

I thought about it and my dream was broken
I clutch at images like dying breath
And I don't want to make a fuss about it
The only certain thing in life is death

Take a look at my new toy
It'll blow your head in two, oh boy

Truth hits everybody
Truth hits everyone
Oh, oh, oh
Truth hits everybody
Truth hits everyone
Truth hits everybody
Truth hits everyone

Where you want to be
Won't you ever see

Truth hits everybody
Truth hits everyone
Oh, oh, oh
Truth hits everybody
Truth hits everyone
Truth hits everybody
Truth hits everyone
Truth hits everybody
Truth hits everyone
Now

Friday 22nd *November 1963. I was twelve years old, in my first year at grammar school, and was watching* The Dick Van Dyke Show *with my mum. Dick was having one of his exasperated arguments with Mary Tyler Moore when the program is interrupted by a news flash from Dallas, Texas.*

Through her tears my mother blamed the communists for the assassination of President Kennedy, but I was sceptical even then: Why would the communists want to do that? Having gotten over my terror of nuclear Armageddon during the Cuban Missile Crisis, I'd actually grown quite fond of Mr. Khrushchev. The image of him hammering the table with his shoe at the UN was such a vibrant contrast to the staid old-world decorum of our own leader, Mr. Macmillan. Strange how a remembered incident from your life can sometimes become the first line of a song.

Born in the '50s

We were born
Born in the fifties
Born
Born in the fifties
Born
Born in the fifties
Born
Born in the fifties

My mother cried
When President Kennedy died
She said it was the communists
But I knew better

Would they drop the bomb on us
While we made love on the beach
We were the class they couldn't teach
'Cos we knew better

We were born
Born in the fifties
Born
Born in the fifties
Born
Born in the fifties
Born
Born in the fifties

They screamed
When the Beatles sang
And they laughed when the King fell down the stairs
Oh they should've known better

Oh we hated our aunt
Then we messed in our pants
Then we lost our faith and prayed to the TV
Oh we should've known better

We were born
Born in the fifties
Born
Born in the fifties
Born
Born in the fifties
Born
Born in the fifties

We freeze like statues on the pages of history
Living was never like this when we took all those G.C.E.'s
Oh you opened the door for us
And then you turned to dust

You don't understand us
So don't reprimand us
We're taking the future
We don't need no teacher

We were born
Born in the fifties
Born
Born in the fifties
Born
Born in the fifties
Born
Born in the fifties

Visions of the Night

Gazed into the visions of the night
Seen the darkness fall
I've heard a mountain fall away from sight
Heard the thunder call

I have seen the beast I call myself
Creature of the night
I feel the creeping darkness close
That I need electric light

They say the meek shall inherit the earth
How long will you keep it?
They sow a harvest but what's it worth?
There's no one left to reap it

Gazed into the visions of the night
Seen the darkness fall
I've heard a mountain fall away from sight
Heard the thunder call

I have seen the beast I call myself
Creature of the night
I feel the creeping darkness close
That I need electric light

They say the meek shall inherit the earth
How long will you keep it?
They sow a harvest but what's it worth?
There's no one left to reap it

Gazed into the visions of the night
Gazed into the visions of the night
Gazed into the visions of the night
Gazed into the visions of the night

They say the meek shall inherit the earth
How long will you keep it?
They sow a harvest but what's it worth?
There's no one left to reap it

Gazed into the visions of the night
Gazed into the visions of the night
Gazed into the visions of the night
Gazed into the visions of the night

I have gazed into the visions of the night
I have gazed into the visions of the night

Message in a Bottle

It's Alright for You

Bring on the Night

Deathwish

Walking on the Moon

The Bed's Too Big Without You

No Time This Time

_____

We recorded our second album in much the same way as our first, even though we'd had some chart success with "Roxanne" and "Can't Stand Losing You" and a successful tour of the U.S. under our belts. We used the same studio, although by now we could afford the day rate and brand-new multitrack tapes. I suppose we were a little superstitious about our good fortune and didn't want to change things too much.

I'd been carrying this guitar riff around in my head for a year. I used to play it over and over again to my dog in our basement flat in Bayswater, and he would stare at me with that look of hopeless resignation dogs can have when they're waiting for their walk in the park. Was it that hopeless look that provoked the idea of the island castaway and his bottle? I don't know, but the song sounded like a hit the first time we played it. The dog finally got his walk, and this song was our first number-one in the UK.

I was pleased that I'd managed a narrative song with a beginning, a middle, and some kind of philosophical resolution in the final verse. If I'd been a more sophisticated songwriter, I would have probably illuminated this change of mood by modulating the third verse into a different key. But it worked anyway.

Message in a Bottle

Just a castaway, an island lost at sea, oh
Another lonely day, with no one here but me, oh
More loneliness than any man could bear
Rescue me before I fall into despair, oh

I'll send an S.O.S. to the world
I'll send an S.O.S. to the world
I hope that someone gets my
I hope that someone gets my
I hope that someone gets my
Message in a bottle, yeah
Message in a bottle, yeah

A year has passed since I wrote my note
But I should have known this right from the start
Only hope can keep me together
Love can mend your life but
Love can break your heart
I'll send an S.O.S. to the world
I'll send an S.O.S. to the world

I hope that someone gets my
I hope that someone gets my
I hope that someone gets my
Message in a bottle, yeah
Message in a bottle, yeah
Message in a bottle, yeah
Message in a bottle, yeah

Walked out this morning, don't believe what I saw
Hundred billion bottles washed up on the shore
Seems I'm not alone at being alone
Hundred billion castaways, looking for a home
I'll send an S.O.S. to the world
I'll send an S.O.S. to the world
I hope that someone gets my
I hope that someone gets my
I hope that someone gets my
Message in a bottle, yeah
Message in a bottle, yeah
Message in a bottle, yeah
Message in a bottle, yeah

Sending out an S.O.S.
Sending out an S.O.S.
Sending out an S.O.S.
Sending out an S.O.S. . . .

It's Alright for You

Wake up
Make up
Bring it up
Shake up
Stand by
Don't cry
Watching while the world dies

Big car
Movie star
Hot tip
Go far
Blind date
Too late
Take a bus
Don't wait

It's alright for you
It's alright for you
It's alright for you
For you and you and you and you and you

It's alright for you
It's alright for you
It's alright for you
For you and you and you

Limp wrist
Tight fist
Contact
No twist
Black dress
No mess
People want no less, no less

Stand by
Don't cry
Watching while the world dies

Three lane
Fast lane
Standing in the cold rain

It's alright for you
It's alright for you
It's alright for you
For you and you and you and you and you

It's alright for you
It's alright for you
It's alright for you
For you

Headlight
High life
Can't sleep
Good night
Up tight
Big fight
Big deal
Too right, too right

Big town
Don't drown
Jump back
Turn around
No life
Flick knife
Finish off my life

It's alright for you
It's alright for you
It's alright for you
For you and you and you and you and you

It's alright for you
It's alright for you
It's alright for you
For you

This was another guitar riff I was deeply proud of but unable to find a home for. The dog was hopelessly resigned about his walk this time as well, so the song ended up as another one about longing.

The second line was shamelessly lifted from T. S. Eliot's "The Love Song of J. Alfred Prufrock."

What was it Eliot said? "Bad poets borrow, good poets steal"?

Bring on the Night

The afternoon has gently passed me by
The evening spreads itself against the sky
Waiting for tomorrow, just another day
As I bid yesterday good-bye

Bring on the night
I couldn't spend another hour of daylight
Bring on the night
I couldn't stand another hour of daylight

The future is but a question mark
Hangs above my head, there in the dark
Can't see for the brightness is staring me blind
As I bid yesterday good-bye

Bring on the night
I couldn't spend another hour of daylight
Bring on the night
I couldn't stand another hour of daylight

I couldn't spend another hour of daylight
I couldn't stand another hour of daylight

Deathwish

Deathwish in the fading light
Headlight pointing through the night
Never thought I'd see the day
Playing with my life this way

Gotta keep my foot right down
If I had wings I'd leave the ground
Burning in the outside lane
People think that I'm insane

The day I take a bend too fast
Judgment that could be my last
I'll be wiped right off the slate
Don't wait up 'cause I'll be late

I'll be late . . .

Couldn't sleep. I was lying in bed in a hotel room in Munich, with this boom ba boom *bass line* running in my head. I scribbled the rhythm down in my notebook, guessing at the notes—C C D F E C—hoping I would be able to make sense of my hieroglyphics the next morning.

I came up with a melody that felt light and airy—in fact, lighter than air. Nine years before, Neil Armstrong had walked on the moon and said the famous words that everyone misquotes. "Giant Steps" is also one of my favorite John Coltrane tunes. Songs are built by whimsy, faulty memory, and free association.

Walking on the Moon

Giant steps are what you take
Walking on the moon
I hope my legs don't break
Walking on the moon
We could walk forever
Walking on the moon
We could live together
Walking on, walking on the moon

Walking back from your house
Walking on the moon
Walking back from your house
Walking on the moon
Feet they hardly touch the ground
Walking on the moon
My feet don't hardly make no sound
Walking on, walking on the moon

Some may say
I'm wishing my days away, no way
And if it's the price I pay, some say
Tomorrow's another day, you'll stay
I may as well play

Giant steps are what you take
Walking on the moon
I hope my legs don't break
Walking on the moon
We could walk forever
Walking on the moon
We could be together
Walking on, walking on the moon

Some may say
I'm wishing my days away, no way
And if it's the price I pay, some say
Tomorrow's another day, you'll stay
I may as well play

The Bed's Too Big Without You

Bed's too big without you
Cold wind blows right through my open door
I can't sleep with your memory
Dreaming dreams of what used to be
When she left I was cold inside
That look on my face was just pride
No regrets, no love, no tears
Living on my own was the least of my fears

Bed's too big without you
The bed's too big without you
The bed's too big without you

Since that day when you'd gone
Just had to carry on
I get through the day, but late at night
Made love to my pillow, but it didn't feel right

Every day just the same
Old rules for the same old game
All I gained was heartache
All I made was one mistake
Now the bed's too big without you
The bed's too big without you
The bed's too big without you

No Time This Time

No time for complexities, the niceties of conversation
No time for smiles, no time for knowing
No less time for intricacies of explanation
No less time for sharing, even less for showing

If I could, I'd slow the whole world down
I'd bring it to its knees
I'd stop it spinning round
But as it is, I'm climbing up an endless wall

No time at all
No time this time
No time at all
No time this time

No time for a quick kiss at the railway station
No time for a suitcase, sandwich and a morning paper
Only time for timetable calls and transportation
No time to think, no time to dare

If I could, I'd slow the whole world down
I'd bring it to its knees
I'd stop it spinning round
But as it is, I'm climbing up an endless wall

No time at all
No time this time
No time at all
No time this time

If I could, I'd slow the whole world down
I'd bring it to its knees
I'd stop it spinning round
But as it is, I'm climbing up an endless wall

No time at all
No time this time
No time at all
No time this time . . .

Don't Stand So Close to Me

Driven to Tears

When the World Is Running Down,
    You Make the Best of What's Still Around

Canary in a Coalmine

Voices Inside My Head

De Do Do Do, De Da Da Da

Man in a Suitcase

Shadows in the Rain

I wrote almost all of these songs in the west of Ireland in 1980. We had a house there, in the village of Roundstone near Clifden in Connemara, County Galway—the most westerly point in Europe. The house was situated on an acre of land, with a well-cared-for garden with a long lawn, mature trees, and an artichoke plant, protected from the ocean by a high seawall. The views were spectacular across the bay to the distant mountains. My basement at home in London had no view at all, a few dustbins, and a stairwell, and now, suddenly, this.

I worked every day after a bracing walk in the Irish air. When I thought I had enough songs, I drove my VW to Dublin and hired a little studio where I could demo my ditties for presentation to the band.

Yes, I was a schoolteacher. No, the song is not auto-biographical!

There are no rules about how to write a song, but one method I often use is the work-backward method. I pluck a title from the air, just free-associating, and then try to figure out a story that it could apply to.

I'm interested in obsession, and Vladimir Nabokov's Lolita is a fascinating study in dangerous obsession. I transposed this idea to a relationship between a teacher and his pupil. Wanting by this time to identify whatever my sources were, I conspired to get the author's name into the song with one of the loosest rhymes in the history of pop. Well, I thought it was hilarious, but I caught some flak.

Don't Stand So Close to Me

Young teacher, the subject
Of schoolgirl fantasy
She wants him so badly
Knows what she wants to be
Inside her there's longing
This girl's an open page
Book marking—she's so close now
This girl is half his age

Don't stand, don't stand so
Don't stand so close to me
Don't stand, don't stand so
Don't stand so close to me

Her friends are so jealous
You know how bad girls get
Sometimes it's not so easy
To be the teacher's pet
Temptation, frustration
So bad it makes him cry
Wet bus stop, she's waiting
His car is warm and dry

Don't stand, don't stand so
Don't stand so close to me
Don't stand, don't stand so
Don't stand so close to me

Loose talk in the classroom
To hurt they try and try
Strong words in the staff room
The accusations fly
It's no use, he sees her
He starts to shake and cough
Just like the old man in
That book by Nabokov

Don't stand, don't stand so
Don't stand so close to me
Don't stand, don't stand so
Don't stand so close to me
Don't stand, don't stand so
Don't stand so close to me

I sang this song at the Live 8 concert in London in 2005, and it seemed as relevant to me then as it was a quarter of a century ago. Biafra, Darfur . . . the issues surrounding genocide are the same, and I wonder if we are making any progress at all, or are we now totally immune to the images of horror that appear daily, everywhere we turn?

Driven to Tears

How can you say that you're not responsible?
What does it have to do with me?
What is my reaction?
What should it be?
Confronted by this latest atrocity
Driven to tears
Driven to tears
Driven to tears

Hide my face in my hands, shame wells in my throat
My comfortable existence is reduced
To a shallow, meaningless party
Seems that when some innocents die
All we can offer them is a page in some magazine
Too many cameras and not enough food
'Cause this is what we've seen
Driven to tears
Driven to tears
Driven to tears

Protest is futile
Nothing seems to get through
What's to become of our world?
Who knows what to do?
Driven to tears
Driven to tears
Driven to tears
Driven to tears
Driven to tears
Driven to tears

I swear I had my tongue firmly in my cheek when I composed this misanthropic, postapocalyptic vision. I imagined a solitary future eking out my days with canned food, a VCR, and old tapes of James Brown and Otis Redding. How many of us have these Robinson Crusoe fantasies of surviving some sort of holocaust? Whereas our survival can only be a collective effort.

When the World Is Running Down, You Make the Best of What's Still Around

Turn on my VCR, same one I've had for years
James Brown on *The T.A.M.I. Show*
Same tape I've had for years
I sit in my old car, same one I've had for years
Old battery's running down, it ran for years and years

Turn on the radio, the static hurts my ears
Tell me, where would I go? I ain't been out in years
Turn on the stereo, it's played for years and years
An Otis Redding song, it's all I own

When the world is running down
You make the best of what's still around
When the world is running down
You make the best of what's still around

Plug in my MCI, to exercise my brain
Make records on my own, can't go out in the rain
Pick up the telephone, I've listened here for years
No one to talk to me, I've listened here for years

When the world is running down
You make the best of what's still around
When the world is running down
You make the best of what's still around

When I feel lonely here, don't waste my time with tears
I run *Deep Throat* again, it ran for years and years
Don't like the food I eat, the cans are running out
Same food for years and years, I hate the food I eat

When the world is running down
You make the best of what's still around
When the world is running down
You make the best of what's still around
When the world is running down
You make the best of what's still around
When the world is running down
You make the best of what's still around

Canary in a Coalmine

First to fall over when the atmosphere is less than perfect
Your sensibilities are shaken by the slightest defect
You live your life like a canary in a coalmine
You get so dizzy even walking in a straight line

You say you want to spend the winter in Firenze
You're so afraid to catch a dose of influenza
You live your life like a canary in a coalmine
You get so dizzy even walking in a straight line

Canary in a coalmine
Canary in a coalmine
Canary in a coalmine

Now if I tell you that you suffer from delusions
You pay your analyst to reach the same conclusions
You live your life like a canary in a coalmine
You get so dizzy even walking in a straight line

Canary in a coalmine
Canary in a coalmine
Canary in a coalmine

First to fall over when the atmosphere is less than perfect
Your sensibilities are shaken by the slightest defect
You live your life like a canary in a coalmine
You get so dizzy even walking in a straight line

Canary in a coalmine
Canary in a coalmine
Canary in a coalmine
Canary in a coalmine . . .

A guy rushed me in Heathrow Airport one day, wild-eyed and breathless. "Hey, man! That song what you wrote, 'Voices inside my head, echoes of things that you said.'"

"Er, yes," I replied, somewhat abashed and looking for my gate number.

"Who is 'you'?" he inquired.

I really didn't know what to say to him, but we stared at each other for what seemed like a long time. Then, as my plane was called, I muttered an apology and started to walk away.

Looking 'round, I saw he was still staring at me and shouting down the length of the concourse: "Who is 'you,' brother? Who is 'you'?"

I smiled weakly at my curious fellow travelers, the challenging koan ringing in my ears, and resolved that I'd have to be less vague in whatever I wrote in future. Somebody somewhere might be taking me seriously.

Voices Inside My Head

Voices inside my head
Echoes of things that you said
Voices inside my head
Echoes of things that you said
Voices inside my head
Echoes of things that you said
Voices inside my head
Echoes of things that you said

I was trying to write an articulate song about being inarticulate. I had always been intrigued by songs like *"Da Doo Ron Ron," "Do Wah Diddy Diddy," "Be Bop a Lula,"* and *"Tutti Frutti."* There was an innocence about them. They weren't trying to be coherent. The lyrics were just pure sound.

Of course, trying to explain this in a song was self-defeating, but I probably learn more from my mistakes than my successes.

De Do Do Do, De Da Da Da

Don't think me unkind
Words are hard to find
They're only cheques I've left unsigned
From the banks of chaos in my mind
And when their eloquence escapes me
Their logic ties me up and rapes me

De do do do, de da da da
Is all I want to say to you
De do do do, de da da da
Their innocence will pull me through
De do do do, de da da da
Is all I want to say to you
De do do do, de da da da
They're meaningless and all that's true

Poets, priests and politicians
Have words to thank for their positions
Words that scream for your submission
And no one's jamming their transmission
And when their eloquence escapes you
Their logic ties you up and rapes you

De do do do, de da da da
Is all I want to say to you
De do do do, de da da da
Their innocence will pull me through

De do do do, de da da da
Is all I want to say to you
De do do do, de da da da
They're meaningless and all that's true

De do do do, de da da da
Is all I want to say to you
De do do do, de da da da
Their innocence will pull me through
De do do do, de da da da
Is all I want to say to you
De do do do, de da da da
They're meaningless and all that's true

Okay, this one is autobiographical. I've spent the last thirty years living in hotels. I can't even unpack when I get home. My suitcase just sits there in the corner of the room, sullen and accusatory, like my old dog.

Man in a Suitcase

I'd invite you back to my place
It's only mine because it holds my suitcase
It looks like home to me alright
But it's a hundred miles from yesterday night

Must I be the man in a suitcase
Is it me, the man with the stranger's face
Must I be the man in a suitcase
Is it me, the man with the stranger's face

Another key for my collection
For security I race for my connection
Bird in a flying cage you'll never get to know me well
The world's my oyster, a hotel room's a prison cell

Must I be the man in a suitcase
Is it me, the man with the stranger's face
Must I be the man in a suitcase
Is it me, the man with the stranger's face

I'd invite you back to my place
It's only mine because it holds my suitcase
It looks like home to me alright
But it's a hundred miles from yesterday night

Must I be the man in a suitcase
Is it me, the man with the stranger's face
Must I be the man in a suitcase
Is it me, the man with the stranger's face

Must I be the man in a suitcase
Is it me, the man with the stranger's face
Must I be the man in a suitcase
Is it me, the man with the stranger's face

Shadows in the Rain

Woke up in my clothes again this morning
I don't know exactly where I am
And I should heed my doctor's warning
He does the best with me he can
He claims I suffer from delusion
But I'm so confident I'm sane
It can't be an optical illusion
So how can you explain
Shadows in the rain

And if you see us on the corner
We're just dancing in the rain
I tell my friends there when I see them
Outside my windowpane
Shadows in the rain
I woke up in my clothes again this morning
I don't know exactly where I am
And I should heed my doctor's warning
He does the best with me he can

He claims I suffer from delusion
But I'm so confident I'm sane
It can't be an optical illusion
So how can you explain
Shadows in the rain

And if you see us on the corner
We're just dancing in the rain
I tell my friends there when I see them
Outside my windowpane
Shadows in the rain

Spirits in the Material World

Every Little Thing She Does Is Magic

Invisible Sun

Hungry for You *(J'aurai toujours faim de toi)*

Demolition Man

Too Much Information

Rehumanize Yourself

One World (Not Three)

Secret Journey

◆

Low Life

I Burn for You

Apart from "Every Little Thing She Does Is Magic," all of the songs on this album were written in the west of Ireland in 1981.

I borrowed the title from Arthur Koestler's 1967 book about the human mind and our seeming appetite for self-destruction. The book talks about how the modern brain of Homo sapiens is grafted onto older and more-primitive prototypes and how in certain situations these reptilian modes of thinking can rise up and overcome our higher modes of logic and reason. I tried, as far as it was possible in a collection of pop songs, to deal with some of these issues. Violence in Northern Ireland in "Invisible Sun," skinheads and Nazis in

"Rehumanize Yourself," destructive pathology in "Demolition Man," lust in "Hungry for You."

The album was densely layered with multitracked vocals, synthesized keyboards, and horn riffs played by yours truly. I wanted to create the impression of something struggling to the surface, something hidden in the recesses of the mind, something from our dark subconscious wanting to be seen. The album cover showed our three faces transposed into digital images, red LED lights on a black background. We were the ghosts in the machine, and while some of the songs are a plea for sanity, others are an expression of that malevolent darkness that haunts us all.

I thought that while political progress is clearly important in resolving conflict around the world, there are spiritual (as opposed to religious) aspects of our recovery that also need to be addressed. I suppose by "spiritual" I mean the ability to see the bigger picture, to be able to step outside the narrow box of our conditioning and access those higher modes of thinking that Koestler talked about.

Without this, politics is just the rhetoric of failure.

Spirits in the Material World

There is no political solution
To our troubled evolution
Have no faith in constitution
There is no bloody revolution

We are spirits in the material world
Are spirits in the material world
Are spirits in the material world
Are spirits in the material world

Our so-called leaders speak
With words they try to jail you
They subjugate the meek
But it's the rhetoric of failure

We are spirits in the material world
Are spirits in the material world
Are spirits in the material world
Are spirits in the material world

Where does the answer lie?
Living from day to day
If it's something we can't buy
There must be another way

We are spirits in the material world
Are spirits in the material world
Are spirits in the material world
Are spirits in the material world

This song was included to try and leaven the rather sober tone of the rest of the record. It was written in 1976, the year I moved to London. I had no money, no prospects, nowhere to live. All I had was Stewart Copeland's phone number and some vague idea of forming a band. It was the year of the Sex Pistols, punk rock, aggressive loud music, violent lyrics, and "Anarchy in the UK." And I wrote this song, which tells you how in touch with the times I was.

Every Little Thing She Does Is Magic

Though I've tried before to tell her
Of the feelings I have for her in my heart
Every time that I come near her
I just lose my nerve as I've done from the start

Every little thing she does is magic
Everything she do just turns me on
Even though my life before was tragic
Now I know my love for her goes on

Do I have to tell the story
Of a thousand rainy days since we first met
It's a big enough umbrella
But it's always me that ends up getting wet

Every little thing she does is magic
Everything she do just turns me on
Even though my life before was tragic
Now I know my love for her goes on

I resolved to call her up
A thousand times a day
And ask her if she'll marry me
In some old-fashioned way
But my silent fears have gripped me
Long before I reach the phone
Long before my tongue has tripped me
Must I always be alone?

Every little thing she does is magic
Everything she do just turns me on
Even though my life before was tragic
Now I know my love for her goes on
Every little thing she does is magic
Everything she do just turns me on
Even though my life before was tragic
Now I know my love for her goes on
Oh yeah, oh yeah, oh yeah

Every little thing, every little thing
Every little thing, every little thing
Every li'le, every li'le, every li'le
Every little thing she does
Every little thing, every little thing
Every little thing, every little thing
Every li'le, every li'le, every li'le
Every little thing she does

The early '80s was an uncomfortable time to be an *Englishman in the west of Ireland. The IRA hunger strikes were taking place across the border, in the north, and feelings were running high. I'd spent some time in Belfast in the mid-'70s, and whenever we took a cab into town, I was told to keep my mouth shut. I looked too much like a "squadie," and my English accent sealed it.*

"Invisible Sun" is a dark, brooding song about the lurking violence of those streets, patrolled by armored cars, haunted by fear and suspicion, and wounds that would take generations to heal. I'm happy that the glimmer of hope in the song's title was somewhat prophetic and pray that the sectarian violence that destroyed so many lives is well and truly over.

Invisible Sun

I don't want to spend the rest of my life
Looking at the barrel of an Armalite
I don't want to spend the rest of my days
Keeping out of trouble like the soldiers say

I don't want to spend my time in hell
Looking at the walls of a prison cell
I don't ever want to play the part
Of a statistic on a government chart

There has to be an invisible sun
It gives its heat to everyone
There has to be an invisible sun
That gives us hope when the whole day's done

It's dark all day, and it glows all night
Factory smoke and acetylene light
I face the day with me head caved in
Looking like something that the cat brought in

There has to be an invisible sun
It gives its heat to everyone
There has to be an invisible sun
That gives us hope when the whole day's done

And they're only going to change this place by
Killing everybody in the human race
And they would kill me for a cigarette
But I don't even wanna die just yet

There has to be an invisible sun
It gives its heat to everyone
There has to be an invisible sun
It gives us hope when the whole day's done

Lust, impure and simple. Trudie helped me with
the French and a lot of the passion.

Hungry for You

(J'aurai toujours faim de toi)

Rien de dormir cette nuit
Je veux de toi
Jusqu'à ce que je sois sec
Mais nos corps sont tous mouillés
Complètement couverts de sueur
Nous nous noyons dans la marée
Je n'ai aucun désir
Tu as ravagé mon coeur
Et moi j'ai bu ton sang
Mais nous pouvons faire ce que nous voulons
J'aurai toujours faim de toi
Mais nous pouvons faire ce que nous voulons
J'aurai toujours faim de toi

Tout le monde est à moi
Je l'ai gagné dans un jeu de cartes
Et maintenant je m'en fous
C'était gagné trop facilement
Ça y est alors, ma belle traîtresse
Il faut que je brûle de jalousie
Tu as ravagé mon coeur
Et moi j'ai bu ton sang
Mais nous pouvons faire ce que nous voulons
J'aurai toujours faim de toi
Mais nous pouvons faire ce que nous voulons
J'aurai toujours faim de toi

Mais nous pouvons faire ce que nous voulons
J'aurai toujours faim de toi
Mais nous pouvons faire ce que nous voulons
J'aurai toujours faim de toi

No matter what I do
I'm still hungry for you
No matter what I do
I'm still hungry for you

Rien de dormir cette nuit
Je veux de toi jusqu'à ce que je sois sec
Mais nos corps sont tous mouillés
Complètement couverts de sueur

I'm hungry for you
I'm hungry for you
I'm still hungry for you
I'm hungry for
I'm hungry for you

A "three-line whip" is a parliamentary expression indicating matters of the utmost seriousness. When I wrote this song, I quite fancied myself as a national emergency. I, too, at times have occasionally indulged in violent revenge fantasies for unspecified slights to my ego, my masculine pride, my patriotism.

Demolition Man

Oh! Demolition, demolition
Demolition, demolition

Tied to the tracks and the train's fast coming
Strapped to the wing with the engine running
You say that this wasn't in your plan
And don't mess around with the demolition man

Tied to a chair and the bomb is ticking
This situation was not of your picking
You say that this wasn't in your plan
And don't mess around with the demolition man

I'm a walking nightmare, an arsenal of doom
I kill conversation as I walk into the room
I'm a three-line whip, I'm the sort of thing they ban
I'm a walking disaster, I'm a demolition man
Demolition, demolition
Demolition, demolition

You come to me like a moth to the flame
It's love you need but I don't play that game
'Cause you could be my greatest fan
But I'm nobody's friend, I'm a demolition man

I'm a walking nightmare, an arsenal of doom
I kill conversation as I walk into the room
I'm a three-line whip, I'm the sort of thing they ban
I'm a walking disaster, I'm a demolition man

Demolition, demolition
Demolition, demolition

Tied to the tracks and the train's fast coming
Strapped to the wing with the engine running
You say that this wasn't in your plan
And don't mess around with the demolition man

Tied to a chair and the bomb is ticking
This situation was not of your picking
You say that this wasn't in your plan
And don't mess around with the demolition man

Too Much Information

Too much information running through my brain
Too much information driving me insane
Too much information running through my brain
Too much information driving me insane

I've seen the whole world six times over
Sea of Japan to the Cliffs of Dover
I've seen the whole world six times over
Sea of Japan to the Cliffs of Dover

Overkill, overview
Over my dead body
Over me, over you
Over everybody

Too much information running through my brain
Too much information driving me insane
Too much information running through my brain
Too much information driving me insane

I've seen the whole world six times over
Sea of Japan to the Cliffs of Dover
I've seen the whole world six times over
Sea of Japan to the Cliffs of Dover

Overkill, overview
Over my dead body
Over me, over you
Over everybody

Too much information running through my brain
Too much information driving me insane
Too much information running through my brain
Too much information driving me insane

A young man was kicked to death by a gang of skinheads near my home. It was around the time my first son was born. When you become a father for the first time, peace and nonviolence becomes even more of an imperative.

Rehumanize Yourself

He goes out at night with his big boots on
None of his friends know right from wrong
They kick a boy to death 'cause he don't belong
You've got to humanize yourself

A policeman put on his uniform
He'd like to have a gun just to keep him warm
Because violence here is a social norm
You've got to humanize yourself

Rehumanize yourself
Rehumanize yourself
Rehumanize yourself
Rehumanize yourself

I work all day at the factory
I'm building a machine that's not for me
There must be a reason that I can't see
You've got to humanize yourself

Billy's joined the National Front
He always was (just) a little runt
He's got his hand in the air with the other cunts
You've got to humanize yourself

Rehumanize yourself
Rehumanize yourself
Rehumanize yourself
Rehumanize yourself

I work all day at the factory
I'm building a machine that's not for me
There must be a reason that I can't see
You've got to humanize yourself

A policeman put on his uniform
He'd like to have a gun just to keep him warm
Because violence here is a social norm
You've got to humanize yourself

Rehumanize yourself
Rehumanize yourself
Rehumanize yourself
Rehumanize yourself . . .

I'd always thought that the term third world *was little more than a semantic trick, treating our poorest neighbors as if they existed on another planet. We are responsible for one another ethically, morally, socially, financially, and in every other sense.*

One World (Not Three)

One world is enough, for all of us
One world is enough, for all of us

It's a subject we rarely mention
But when we do we have this little invention
By pretending they're a different world from me
I show my responsibility
One world is enough, for all of us
One world is enough, for all of us

The third world breathes our air tomorrow
We live on the time we borrow
In our world there's no time for sorrow
In their world there is no tomorrow
One world is enough, for all of us
One world is enough, for all of us

Lines are drawn upon the world
Before we get our flags unfurled
Whichever one we pick
It's just a self-deluding trick
One world is enough, for all of us
One world is enough, for all of us

I don't want to bring a sour note
Remember this before you vote
We can all sink or we all float
'Cause we're all in the same big boat
One world is enough for all of us

One world is enough for all of us
One world is enough for all of us
One world is enough for all of us
It may seem a million miles away
But it gets a little closer every day
It may seem a million miles away
But it gets a little closer every day

I was intrigued by G. I. Gurdjieff's Meetings with Remarkable Men, *his account of the travels and discoveries of an intrepid group of spiritual adventurers. I was looking for some spiritual guidance for my own life and, after a few false leads, finally began to listen to the discrete language of my own heart.*

Secret Journey

Upon a secret journey
I met a holy man
His blindness was his wisdom
I'm such a lonely man

And as the world was turning
It rolled itself in pain
This does not seem to touch you
He pointed to the rain

You will see light in the darkness
You will make some sense of this
And when you've made your secret journey
You will find this love you miss

And on the days that followed
I listened to his words
I strained to understand him
I chased his thoughts like birds

You will see light in the darkness
You will make some sense of this
And when you've made your secret journey
You will find this love you miss

You will see light in the darkness
You will make some sense of this
You will see joy in this sadness
You will find this love you miss

And when you've made your secret journey
You will be a holy man
And when you've made your secret journey
You will be a holy man . . .

Low Life

Fatal fascination for the seedy part of town
Walk down the street and your head spins round
Don't be seen alone without your friends at night
Take a gun or a knife to the low life

Don't have to be born into this society
Pay for love but the hate comes free
Bring enough money for the rest of your life
Don't bring your wife to the low life

Bringing us there to the degradation
Always keep your back to the wall
No rewards for your infatuation
Low life
No life at all

Yeah, low life, low life

In here too long to be afraid anymore
You can't reach the bed so you sleep on the floor
You get so stoned you think you could fly
But you won't get high on the low life

Low life, low life
Low life, low life
Low life, low life
Low life, low life

I Burn for You

Now that I have found you
In the coolth of your evening smile
The shade of your parasol
And your love flows through me
Though I drink at your pool
I burn for you, I burn for

You and I are lovers
When nighttime folds around our bed
In peace we sleep entwined
And your love flows through me
Though an ocean soothes my head
I burn for you, I burn for

Stars will fall from dark skies
As ancient rocks are turning
Quiet fills the room
And your love flows through me
Though I lie here so still
I burn for you, I burn for you

I burn . . .

Synchronicity I

Walking in Your Footsteps

O My God

Synchronicity II

Every Breath You Take

King of Pain

Wrapped Around Your Finger

Tea in the Sahara

Murder by Numbers

◆

Once Upon a Daydream

This was our final studio album. I wrote a lot of these songs in Golden Eye, Ian Fleming's old home on the north shore of Jamaica. Britain had gone to war with Argentina over the Falklands. Young men were dying in the freezing waters of the South Atlantic, while I was gazing at sunspots on a clifftop overlooking the Caribbean. During this time I read Arthur Koestler, whose work in turn led me to Carl Jung. The title of the album refers to Jung's concept of meaningful coincidence

Synchronicity *was recorded on the island of Montserrat in 1983.*

Synchronicity I

With one breath, with one flow
You will know
Synchronicity

A sleep trance, a dream dance
A shared romance
Synchronicity

A connecting principle
Linked to the invisible
Almost imperceptible
Something inexpressible
Science insusceptible
Logic so inflexible
Causally connectible
Yet nothing is invincible

If we share this nightmare
Then we can dream
Spiritus mundi

If you act, as you think
The missing link
Synchronicity

We know you, they know me
Extrasensory
Synchronicity

A star fall, a phone call
It joins all
Synchronicity
It's so deep, it's so wide
You're inside
Synchronicity

Effect without a cause
Subatomic laws,
Scientific pause

Synchronicity . . .

There's a picture of me taken by Duane Michals in the Museum of Natural History in New York. I'm standing inside the rib cage of a dinosaur. It struck me that we were clearly related, albeit separated by a few million years.

Walking in Your Footsteps

Fifty million years ago
You walked upon the planet so
Lord of all that you could see
Just a little bit like me

Walking in your footsteps
Walking in your footsteps
Walking in your footsteps
Walking in your footsteps

Hey, Mr. Dinosaur
You really couldn't ask for more
You were God's favorite creature
But you didn't have a future

Walking in your footsteps
Walking in your footsteps
Walking in your footsteps
Walking in your footsteps

Hey, mighty brontosaurus
Don't you have a message for us
You thought your rule would always last
There were no lessons in your past
You were built three stories high
They say you would not hurt a fly
If we explode the atom bomb
Would they say that we were dumb?

Walking in your footsteps
Walking in your footsteps
Walking in your footsteps
Walking in your footsteps

Fifty million years ago
They walked upon the planet so
They live in a museum
It's the only place you'll see 'em

Walking in your footsteps
Walking in your footsteps

They say the meek shall inherit the earth
They say the meek shall inherit the earth

Walking in your footsteps

I'm told the word religion comes from the Latin ligare, to connect. So I assume religion means to reconnect, and yet more often than not, religions seem to separate us from one another. I've chosen to live my life without the "certainties" of faith, but I do maintain a great reverence for the mystery and wonder of our existence, and my agnosticism is a tolerant cousin to my curiosity.

This song started something of a tradition with me, where I would quote lines from previous songs in the coda. The effect seemed to be disarming and humorous and perhaps unconsciously pointing out that all of these songs are one song really—modular, mutable, and not too serious.

O My God

Everyone I know is lonely
And God's so far away
And my heart belongs to no one
So now sometimes I pray
Please take the space between us
And fill it up some way
Take the space between us
And fill it up some way

O my God, you take the biscuit
Treating me this way
Expecting me to treat you well
No matter what you say
How can I turn the other cheek
It's black and bruised and torn
I've been waiting
Since the day that I was born

Take the space between us
And fill it up some way
Take the space between us
And fill it up some way

The fat man in his garden
The thin man at his gate
My God, you must be sleeping
Wake up, it's much too late

Take the space between us
And fill it up some way
Take the space between us
And fill it up some way

Do I have to tell the story
Of a thousand rainy days
Since we first met?
It's a big enough umbrella
But it's always me that ends up getting wet

This song was an attempt to link a tale of suburban alien-
ation with symbolic events at a distance, i.e., the monster emerging from
a Scottish lake and a domestic melodrama. I was trying to dramatize
Jung's theory of meaningful coincidence, but it was a rocking song
nonetheless!

Synchronicity II

Another suburban family morning
Grandmother screaming at the wall
We have to shout above the din of our Rice Krispies
We can't hear anything at all
Mother chants her litany of boredom and frustration
But we know all her suicides are fake
Daddy only stares into the distance
There's only so much more that he can take
Many miles away
Something crawls from the slime
At the bottom of a dark Scottish lake

Another industrial ugly morning
The factory belches filth into the sky
He walks unhindered through the picket lines today
He doesn't think to wonder why
The secretaries pout and preen like
Cheap tarts in a red-light street
But all he ever thinks to do is watch
And every single meeting with his so-called superior
Is a humiliating kick in the crotch
Many miles away
Something crawls to the surface
Of a dark Scottish lake

Another working day has ended
Only the rush-hour hell to face
Packed like lemmings into shiny metal boxes
Contestants in a suicidal race

Daddy grips the wheel and stares alone into the distance
He knows that something somewhere has to break
He sees the family home now looming in the headlights
The pain upstairs that makes his eyeballs ache
Many miles away
There's a shadow on the door
Of a cottage on the shore
Of a dark Scottish lake

Many miles away, many miles away

I make no claims for any originality in this song. It shares a chord sequence with a million other songs, the melody is nursery-rhyme simple, as are the lyrics, and yet the song has a kind of power. I'd like to think that power lies in its ambiguity, in its being both seductive and sinister.

My original intention was to make it a seductive love song, but what I ended up with was something much darker. My life had invaded the song. Everything around me seemed to be disintegrating: my marriage, my band, my sanity, and this at a time when, from the outside, I appeared to be one of the most successful musicians in the world.

The song has the standard structure of a pop ballad, but there is no harmonic development after the middle eight, no release of emotions or change in the point of view of the protagonist. He is trapped in his circular obsessions. Of course, I wasn't aware of any of this. I thought I was just writing a hit song, and indeed it became one of the songs that defined the '80s, and by accident the perfect sound track for Reagan's Star Wars fantasy of control and seduction.

When I finally became aware of this symmetry, I was forced to write an antidote: "If You Love Somebody Set Them Free."

Every Breath You Take

Every breath you take
And every move you make
Every bond you break, every step you take
I'll be watching you

Every single day
And every word you say
Every game you play, every night you stay
I'll be watching you

Oh, can't you see
You belong to me?
How my poor heart aches

With every step you take
Every move you make
Every vow you break
Every smile you fake, every claim you stake
I'll be watching you

Since you've gone I've been lost without a trace
I dream at night, I can only see your face
I look around, but it's you I can't replace
I feel so cold, and I long for your embrace
I keep crying baby, baby, please

Oh, can't you see
You belong to me?
How my poor heart aches
With every step you take
Every move you make
Every vow you break
Every smile you fake, every claim you stake
I'll be watching you
Every move you make, every step you take
I'll be watching you
I'll be watching you

I was sitting moping under a tree in the garden, and as the sun was sinking toward the western horizon, I noticed that there was a lot of sunspot activity.

I turned to Trudie. "There's a little black spot on the sun today."

She waited expectantly, not really indulging my mood but tolerant.

"That's my soul up there," I added gratuitously.

Trudie discreetly raised her eyes to the heavens. "There he goes again, the king of pain."

King of Pain

There's a little black spot on the sun today
It's the same old thing as yesterday
There's a black hat caught in a high treetop
There's a flagpole rag and the wind won't stop

I have stood here before inside the pouring rain
With the world turning circles running 'round my brain
I guess I'm always hoping that you'll end this reign
But it's my destiny to be the king of pain

There's a little black spot on the sun today
That's my soul up there
It's the same old thing as yesterday
That's my soul up there
There's a black hat caught in a high treetop
That's my soul up there
There's a flagpole rag and the wind won't stop
That's my soul up there

I have stood here before inside the pouring rain
With the world turning circles running 'round my brain
I guess I'm always hoping that you'll end this reign
But it's my destiny to be the king of pain

There's a fossil that's trapped in a high cliff wall
That's my soul up there
There's a dead salmon frozen in a waterfall

That's my soul up there
There's a blue whale beached by a springtime's ebb
That's my soul up there
There's a butterfly trapped in a spider's web
That's my soul up there

I have stood here before inside the pouring rain
With the world turning circles running 'round my brain
I guess I'm always hoping that you'll end this reign
But it's my destiny to be the king of pain

There's a king on a throne with his eyes torn out
There's a blind man looking for a shadow of doubt
There's a rich man sleeping on a golden bed
There's a skeleton choking on a crust of bread

King of pain

There's a red fox torn by a huntsman's pack
That's my soul up there
There's a black-winged gull with a broken back
That's my soul up there
There's a little black spot on the sun today
It's the same old thing as yesterday

I have stood here before in the pouring rain
With the world turning circles running 'round my brain
I guess I always thought you could end this reign
But it's my destiny to be the king of pain

King of pain
King of pain
King of pain
I'll always be king of pain

This song is vaguely alchemical and probably about a friend of mine, a professional psychic and my tutor in tarot, with bits of Doctor Faustus *and* "The Sorcerer's Apprentice" *thrown into the pot for good measure.*

Wrapped Around Your Finger

You consider me the young apprentice
Caught between the Scylla and Charybdis
Hypnotized by you if I should linger
Staring at the ring around your finger

I have only come here seeking knowledge
Things they would not teach me of in college
I can see the destiny you sold
Turned into a shining band of gold

I'll be wrapped around your finger
I'll be wrapped around your finger

Mephistopheles is not your name
But I know what you're up to just the same
I will listen hard to your tuition
And you will see it come to its fruition

I'll be wrapped around your finger
I'll be wrapped around your finger

Devil and the deep blue sea behind me
Vanish in the air, you'll never find me
I will turn your face to alabaster
Then you'll find your servant is your master

You'll be wrapped around my finger
You'll be wrapped around my finger
You'll be wrapped around my finger

This song comes from a story told in The Sheltering Sky, the remarkable novel by Paul Bowles. It involves three sisters who have only one ambition: to drink tea in the Sahara. They dance for money in the cafés of Ghardia, but they are always sad because the Algerian men they dance for are ugly and they don't pay enough money for the sisters to indulge their ambition.

One day a handsome young man asks them to dance, he tells them about his home in the desert, and then he leaves. They have all fallen in love with him.

They save enough money to buy a teapot and some cups, and they set out for the desert to find him. The story ends tragically, of course.

Tea in the Sahara

My sisters and I
Have this wish before we die
And it may sound strange
As if our minds are deranged
Please don't ask us why
Beneath the sheltering sky
We have this strange obsession
You have the means in your possession

We want our tea in the Sahara with you
We want our tea in the Sahara with you

The young man agreed
He would satisfy their need
So they danced for his pleasure
With a joy you could not measure
They would wait for him here
The same place every year
Beneath the sheltering sky
Across the desert he would fly

Tea in the Sahara with you
Tea in the Sahara with you

The sky turned to black
Would he ever come back?
They would climb a high dune
They would pray to the moon
But he'd never return
So the sisters would burn
As their eyes searched the land
With their cups full of sand

Tea in the Sahara with you
Tea in the Sahara with you
Tea in the Sahara with you
Tea in the Sahara with you

Andy brought a set of very jazzy and sophisticated chords into the studio one day, and I asked him if I could write some lyrics to fit them. Then I took myself on a long walk up to the volcano on top of the island with a tape of the chords playing in my head.

A few years later this volcano would destroy half of Montserrat, but on this day it was just bubbling quietly and throwing up a strong smell of sulfur. The words formed in my head and that pungent smell of sulfur continued to cling to the song: Jimmy Swaggart, the TV evangelist, publicly cited it as an example of the devil's work. He condemned it colorfully while entirely missing its irony and its satirical intent.

The devil indeed!

Murder by Numbers

Once that you've decided on a killing
First you make a stone of your heart
And if you find that your hands are still willing
Then you can turn a murder into art

There really isn't any need for bloodshed
You just do it with a little more finesse
If you can slip a tablet into someone's coffee
Then it avoids an awful lot of mess

It's murder by numbers, one, two, three
It's as easy to learn as your ABC
Murder by numbers, one, two, three
It's as easy to learn as your ABC

Now if you have a taste for this experience
And you're flushed with your very first success
Then you must try a twosome or a threesome
And you'll find your conscience bothers you much less

Because murder is like anything you take to
It's a habit-forming need for more and more
You can bump off every member of your family
And anybody else you find a bore

Because it's murder by numbers, one, two, three
It's as easy to learn as your ABC
Murder by numbers, one, two, three
It's as easy to learn as your ABC

Now you can join the ranks of the illustrious
In history's great dark hall of fame
All our greatest killers were industrious
At least the ones that we all know by name

But you can reach the top of your profession
If you become the leader of the land
For murder is the sport of the elected
And you don't need to lift a finger of your hand

Because it's murder by numbers, one, two, three
It's as easy to learn as your ABC
Murder by numbers, one, two, three

Once Upon a Daydream

Once upon a daydream
I fell in love with you
Once upon a moonbeam
I gave that love to you
Once upon a lifetime
I know it must be true
When the months had turned us
I'd have to marry you

Once upon a daydream
Doesn't happen anymore
Once upon a moonbeam
This is no place for tenderness

Once her daddy found out
He threw her to the floor
He killed her unborn baby
And kicked me from the door
Once upon a nightmare
I bought myself a gun
I blew her daddy's brains out
Now hell has just begun

Once upon a daydream
Doesn't happen anymore
Once upon a moonbeam
This is no place for sentiment

Once upon a lifetime
A lifetime filled with tears
The boy would pay for his crime
With all his natural years
Once upon a daydream
He'd make you his someday
Once upon a moonbeam
He'd dream his life away

Once upon a daydream
Doesn't happen anymore
Once upon a moonbeam
This is no place for miracles

Once upon a daydream
Once upon a daydream
Once upon a daydream
Once upon a day . . . dream

If You Love Somebody Set Them Free

Love Is the Seventh Wave

Russians

Children's Crusade

We Work the Black Seam

Consider Me Gone

Moon over Bourbon Street

Fortress Around Your Heart

◆

Another Day

Following the massive success of Synchronicity,
I decided to set out on my own. This decision, I admit, was
not particularly logical. In the eyes of some it was the highest
folly to leave what was arguably the biggest band in the world
at that time.

Of course it was a risk, but I can only say that I listened to
my instincts, no matter how irrational they seemed to everyone
else, and then followed them, fully aware that falling flat on
my face was a very real possibility. I ignored this as much as I
could, believing that the momentum of the band had been
such that people would be at least curious about what I was up
to. I have to say the sense of freedom in not having to tailor
songs to accommodate a three-piece, even one as versatile
as the Police, was like opening a window in a closed room.
Although I believed that the Police had thrived on the

limitations of being a small band, I was more than ready after seven years to fly the coop.

With the help of my friend, the writer and critic Vic Garbarini, I recruited a band of young jazz musicians, including alumni of Miles Davis's band, Art Blakey's band, and Weather Report. Branford Marsalis would play saxophone, with Kenny Kirkland on piano. This caused some friction with Branford's brother, Wynton, who, apart from losing two of his band, thought they were selling out by playing with a pop musician like myself. Nevertheless, we all set out for Eddie Grant's studio in Barbados with a bag full of new songs and a mission to start a new adventure.

The title of the album came from a dream that woke me up on my first night in Barbados. I dreamed I was sitting in the walled garden behind my house in Hampstead, under a lilac tree on a well-manicured lawn, surrounded by beautiful rosebushes. Suddenly the bricks from the wall exploded into the garden and I turned to see the head of an enormous turtle emerging from the darkness, followed by four or five others. They were not only the size of a man, they were also blue and had an air of being immensely cool, like hepcats, insouciant and fearless. They didn't harm me but with an almost casual violence commenced to destroy my genteel English garden, digging up the lawn with their claws, chomping at the rosebushes, bulldozing the lilac tree. Total mayhem. I woke up to the sound of Branford in the room upstairs, riffing wildly on his tenor sax, followed by his unmistakable laughter.

This song was as much a hymn to my newfound freedom as it was an antidote to the brooding issues of control and surveillance that haunted "Every Breath You Take." Perhaps the highest compliment you can pay to a partner is "I don't own you—you're free." If you were to try to possess them in the obvious way, you could never appreciate them in the way that really counts. There are too many prisons in the world already.

If You Love Somebody Set Them Free

Free, free, set them free
Free, free, set them free
Free, free, set them free
If you need somebody
Call my name
If you want someone
You can do the same
If you want to keep something precious
You got to lock it up and throw away the key
If you want to hold on to your possession
Don't even think about me

If you love somebody
If you love someone
If you love somebody
If you love someone, set them free
Set them free
Set them free
Set them free

If it's a mirror you want
Just look into my eyes
Or a whipping boy
Someone to despise
Or a prisoner in the dark
Tied up in chains you just can't see
Or a beast in a gilded cage
That's all some people ever want to be

If you love somebody
If you love someone
If you love somebody
If you love someone, set them free
Set them free
Set them free
Set them free

You can't control an independent heart
Can't tear the one you love apart
Forever conditioned to believe that we can't live
We can't live here and be happy with less
So many riches
So many souls
With everything we see that we want to possess

If you need somebody
Call my name
If you want someone
You can do the same
If you want to keep something precious
You got to lock it up and throw away the key
You want to hold on to your possession
Don't even think about me

If you love somebody
If you love someone
If you love somebody
If you love someone, set them free
Set them free
Set them free
Set them free
Set them free

Love Is the Seventh Wave

In the empire of the senses
You're the queen of all you survey
All the cities, all the nation
Everything that falls your way, I say
There is a deeper world than this that you don't understand
There is a deeper world than this tugging at your hand
Every ripple on the ocean
Every leaf on every tree
Every sand dune in the desert
Every power we never see
There is a deeper wave than this, swelling in the world
There is a deeper wave than this, listen to me, girl

Feel it rising in the cities
Feel it sweeping overland
Over borders, over frontiers
Nothing will its power withstand, I say
There is no deeper wave than this, rising in the world
There is no deeper wave than this, listen to me, girl

All the bloodshed, all the anger
All the weapons, all the greed
All the armies, all the missiles
All the symbols of that fear, I say
There is a deeper wave than this, rising in the world
There is a deeper wave than this, listen to me, girl

At the still point of destruction
At the center of the fury
All the angels, all the devils
All around us, can't you see?
There is a deeper wave than this, rising in the land
There is a deeper wave than this, nothing will withstand

I say love is the seventh wave
I say love is the seventh wave
I say love is the seventh wave

I say love is the seventh wave
I say love is the seventh wave
I say love is the seventh wave
I say love

Every ripple on the ocean
Every leaf on every tree
Every sand dune in the desert
Every breath you take with me
Every breath you take, every move you make
Every cake you bake, every leg you break

We were suffering one of those cyclic chills in the Cold War between the West and the Soviets, this time personified by the belligerent exchanges of Mr. Reagan and Mr. Brezhnev. The president, in the B-movie rhetoric he favored, condemned Russia as the "Evil Empire." To me this sounded like another bad line from Flash Gordon and seemed to do nothing to allay the chronic mistrust between the world's superpowers.

This era of name-calling produced the Rambo movies, where a pathologically violent survivor of Vietnam wreaks terrible vengeance on the faceless enemies of the West. In one of the movies, our hero is embedded with the CIA-supported rebels in Afghanistan, helping, with as much gratuitous violence as possible, to overthrow the tyrannical Russian oppressors. It's ironic that it was exactly this Rambo-style foreign policy that armed and logistically supported Osama bin Laden when he was fighting the Soviets.

In this political climate a friend of mine, who was doing research at Columbia University in New York, had a computer system sophisticated enough to intercept the Soviet's TV signal from their satellite above the North Pole. On a Saturday night in New York City we could watch Sunday morning programs for the kids in Russia. The shows seemed thoughtful and sweet, and I suddenly felt the need to state something obvious in the face of all this rhetoric: Russians love their children just as we do.

Russians

In Europe and America there's a growing feeling of hysteria
Conditioned to respond to all the threats
In the rhetorical speeches of the Soviets
Mister Khrushchev said, "We will bury you"
I don't subscribe to this point of view
It'd be such an ignorant thing to do
If the Russians love their children too

How can I save my little boy
From Oppenheimer's deadly toy?
There is no monopoly on common sense

On either side of the political fence
We share the same biology
Regardless of ideology
Believe me when I say to you
I hope the Russians love their children too

There is no historical precedent to put
Words in the mouth of the president
There's no such thing as a winnable war
It's a lie we don't believe anymore
Mister Reagan says, "We will protect you"
I don't subscribe to this point of view
Believe me when I say to you
I hope the Russians love their children too
We share the same biology
Regardless of ideology
What might save us, me and you
Is if the Russians love their children too

This is one of my more ambitious songs. I tried to combine an abiding interest in the First World War, heroin addiction in contemporary London, and the abuse of twelfth-century street children, who were sold into slavery in a cynical pseudoreligious scam that was appalling even by the low moral standards of the Crusaders and the ethics of the time. There seemed to be a connection.

Children's Crusade

Young men, soldiers, nineteen fourteen
Marching through countries they'd never seen
Virgins with rifles, a game of charades
All for a children's crusade
Pawns in the game are not victims of chance
Strewn on the fields of Belgium and France
Poppies for young men, death's bitter trade
All of those young lives betrayed

The children of England would never be slaves
They're trapped on the wire and dying in waves
The flower of England facedown in the mud
And stained in the blood of a whole generation

Corpulent generals safe behind lines
History's lessons drowned in red wine
Poppies for young men, death's bitter trade
All of those young lives betrayed
All for a children's crusade

The children of England would never be slaves
They're trapped on the wire and dying in waves
The flower of England facedown in the mud
And stained in the blood of a whole generation

Midnight in Soho, nineteen eighty-four
Fixing in doorways, opium slaves
Poppies for young men, such bitter trade
All of those young lives betrayed
All for a children's crusade

The 1984 Miners' Strike in Britain disintegrated
*into a personality clash between the Prime Minister, Mrs. Thatcher, and
the miners' union leader, Arthur Scargill. As I was raised in a mining
community, I felt not a little sympathy for the miners, whose way of life
was being threatened, and also had some serious concerns about the
safety of the nuclear power stations the government was putting such
faith in.*

*Of course, neither source of power is ideal, but that would be another
song.*

We Work the Black Seam

This place has changed for good
Your economic theory said it would
It's hard for us to understand
We can't give up our jobs the way we should
Our blood has stained the coal
We tunneled deep inside the nation's soul
We matter more than pounds and pence
Your economic theory makes no sense

One day in a nuclear age
They may understand our rage
They build machines that they can't control
And bury the waste in a great big hole
Power was to become cheap and clean
Grimy faces were never seen
Deadly for twelve thousand years is carbon fourteen
We work the black seam together
We work the black seam together

The seam lies underground
Three million years of pressure packed it down
We walk through ancient forest lands
And light a thousand cities with our hands
Your dark satanic mills
Have made redundant all our mining skills

You can't exchange a six-inch band
For all the poisoned streams in Cumberland
Your economic theory makes no sense

One day in a nuclear age
They may understand our rage
They build machines that they can't control
And bury the waste in a great big hole
Power was to become cheap and clean
Grimy faces were never seen
Deadly for twelve thousand years is carbon fourteen
We work the black seam together
We work the black seam together

Should the children weep
The turning world will sing their souls to sleep
When you have sunk without a trace
The universe will suck me into place

One day in a nuclear age
They may understand our rage
They build machines that they can't control
And bury the waste in a great big hole
Power was to become cheap and clean
Grimy faces were never seen
But deadly for twelve thousand years is carbon fourteen
We work the black seam together
We work the black seam together

It's nice to be able to use our national bard as a resource,
and "Sonnet XXXV" was always one of my favorites.
I've always fancied this title as my epitaph.

Consider Me Gone

You can't say that!
You can't say that!
You can't say that!
You can't say that!
There were rooms of forgiveness
In the house that we share
But the space has been emptied
Of whatever was there
There were cupboards of patience
There were shelf-loads of care
But whoever came calling
Found nobody there
After today
After today
Consider me gone

You can't say that!
You can't say that!
You can't say that!
You can't say that!

Roses have thorns
Shining water's mud
And cancer lurks deep
In the sweetest bud
Clouds and eclipses
Stain the moon and the sun
And history reeks
Of the wrongs we have done
After today
After today
Consider me gone

I've spent too many years
At war with myself
The doctor has told me
It's no good for my health
To search for perfection
Is all very well
But to look for heaven
Is to live here in hell
After today
After today
After today
Consider me gone
Consider me gone
Consider me, consider me
Consider me gone, gone, gone, gone

Anne Rice's Interview with the Vampire *was the direct inspiration for this song, but there was one moonlit night in the French Quarter of New Orleans where I had the distinct impression that I was being followed.*

Moon over Bourbon Street

There's a moon over Bourbon Street tonight
I see faces as they pass beneath the pale lamplight
I've no choice but to follow that call
The bright lights, the people, and the moon and all
I pray every day to be strong
For I know what I do must be wrong
Oh you'll never see my shade or hear the sound of my feet
While there's a moon over Bourbon Street

It was many years ago that I became what I am
I was trapped in this life like an innocent lamb
Now I can never show my face at noon
And you'll only see me walking by the light of the moon
The brim of my hat hides the eye of a beast
I've the face of a sinner but the hands of a priest
Oh you'll never see my shade or hear the sound of my feet
While there's a moon over Bourbon Street

She walks every day through the streets of New Orleans
She's innocent and young, from a family of means
I have stood many times outside her window at night
To struggle with my instinct in the pale moonlight
How could I be this way when I pray to God above?
I must love what I destroy and destroy the thing I love
Oh you'll never see my shade or hear the sound of my feet
While there's a moon over Bourbon Street

There are songs of love, songs of heartache, songs of revenge. And then there are songs of reconciliation.

Fortress Around Your Heart

Under the ruins of a walled city
Crumbling towers in beams of yellow light
No flags of truce, no cries of pity
The siege guns had been pounding through the night
It took a day to build the city
We walked through its streets in the afternoon
As I returned across the fields I'd known
I recognized the walls that I once made
I had to stop in my tracks for fear
Of walking on the mines I'd laid

And if I've built this fortress around your heart
Encircled you in trenches and barbed wire
Then let me build a bridge
For I cannot fill the chasm
And let me set the battlements on fire

Then I went off to fight some battle
That I'd invented inside my head
Away so long for years and years
You probably thought or even wished that I was dead
While the armies all are sleeping
Beneath the tattered flag we'd made
I had to stop in my tracks for fear
Of walking on the mines I'd laid

And if I've built this fortress around your heart
Encircled you in trenches and barbed wire
Then let me build a bridge
For I cannot fill the chasm
And let me set the battlements on fire

This prison has now become your home
A sentence you seem prepared to pay
It took a day to build the city
We walked through its streets in the afternoon
As I returned across the lands I'd known
I recognized the fields where I'd once played
I had to stop in my tracks for fear
Of walking on the mines I'd laid

And if I've built this fortress around your heart
Encircled you in trenches and barbed wire
Then let me build a bridge
For I cannot fill the chasm
And let me set the battlements on fire

Another Day

Every day that goes by
A new hungry baby starts to cry
Born astride a painful grave
Drowned in hunger's tidal wave
Pick a child that you can save
It'd be the only one

If Africa escapes starvation
Not only food but education
The desert grows with every minute
Trapping everybody in it
All the children look the same
They wonder why they came
But it's hard to tell the poison from the cure
It's harder still to know the reason why, why, why
The only thing I really know for sure
Is that another day, another day's gone by

Every day that goes by
A brand new missile points towards the sky
We're survivors of a game of chance
Beneath an arms race avalanche
If you survive this winter's cold
You'd be the only one

If we escape annihilation
Not only hope but education
The world is ruled by Bellophiles
Adding to their weapon piles
Imagine what your taxes buy
We hardly ever try
But it's hard to tell the poison from the cure
It's harder still to know the reason why, why, why
The only thing I really know for sure
Is that another day, another day's gone by, bye, bye

That this too solid flesh
Would melt and resolve into a dew
Suffocating lassitude
Drowning in my platitude
Trapped by insecurities
I'm not the only one
If I survive this dislocation
Have to use my education

Chief of inactivity
Wasted creativity
Distances our revolution
Silence is consent
But it's hard to tell the poison from the cure
It's harder still to know the reason why, why, why
The only thing I really know for sure
Is that another day, another day's gone by

The Lazarus Heart

Be Still My Beating Heart

Englishman in New York

History Will Teach Us Nothing

They Dance Alone *(Cueca Solo)*

Fragile

We'll Be Together

Straight to My Heart

Rock Steady

Sister Moon

The Secret Marriage

◆

Conversation with a Dog

My mother was terminally ill during the writing of this album and I think this strongly influenced my creative process, not that the record is in the least morbid—my mother would not have wanted to be remembered that way. There is a thread of romance, sadness, and fun that characterizes the record as well as her life.

"Lazarus Heart" was a vivid nightmare that I wrote down and then fashioned into a song.

A learned friend of mine informs me that it is the archetypal dream of The Fisher King. *Can't I do anything original?*

The Lazarus Heart

He looked beneath his shirt today
There was a wound in his flesh so deep and wide
From the wound a lovely flower grew
From somewhere deep inside
He turned around to face his mother
To show her the wound in his breast
That burned like a brand
But the sword that cut him open
Was the sword in his mother's hand

Every day another miracle
Only death will tear us apart
To sacrifice a life for yours
I'd be the blood of the Lazarus heart
The blood of the Lazarus heart

Though the sword was his protection
The wound itself would give him power
The power to remake himself at the time of his darkest hour
She said the wound would give him courage and pain
The kind of pain that you can't hide
From the wound a lovely flower grew
From somewhere deep inside

Every day another miracle
Only death will keep us apart
To sacrifice a life for yours
I'd be the blood of the Lazarus heart
The blood of the Lazarus heart

Birds on the roof of my mother's house
I've no stones that chase them away
Birds on the roof of my mother's house
Will sit on my roof someday
They fly at the window, they fly at the door
Where does she get the strength to fight them anymore
She counts all her children as a shield against the rain
Lifts her eyes to the sky like a flower to the rain

Every day another miracle
Only death will keep us apart
To sacrifice a life for yours
I'd be the blood of the Lazarus heart
The blood of the Lazarus heart

Be Still My Beating Heart

Be still my beating heart
It would be better to be cool
It's not time to be open just yet
A lesson once learned is so hard to forget
Be still my beating heart
Or I'll be taken for a fool
It's not healthy to run at this pace
The blood runs so red to my face
I've been to every single book I know
To soothe the thoughts that plague me so
I sink like a stone that's been thrown in the ocean
My logic has drowned in a sea of emotion
Stop before you start
Be still my beating heart

Restore my broken dreams
Shattered like a falling glass
I'm not ready to be broken just yet
A lesson once learned is so hard to forget

Be still my beating heart
You must learn to stand your ground
It's not healthy to run at this pace
The blood runs so red to my face
I've been to every single book I know
To soothe the thoughts that plague me so
Stop before you start
Be still my beating heart

Never to be wrong
Never to make promises that break
It's like singing in the wind
Or writing on the surface of a lake
And I wriggle like a fish caught on dry land
And I struggle to avoid any help at hand

I sink like a stone that's been thrown in the ocean
My logic has drowned in a sea of emotion
Stop before you start
Be still my beating heart

I've kept an apartment in New York since the mid-'80s. There are lots of English people there, but you wouldn't notice us. We assimilate very well into the life of the city, seeming to prefer our singular anonymity. The only places you'll find us in any numbers, however, are in the English pubs spread discreetly around Manhattan.

When I first moved to New York and felt homesick, I'd go, early on Saturday mornings, to one of these pubs to watch live soccer from England via satellite. There you could drink English beer, enjoy a greasy fried breakfast, and rub shoulders with Englishmen from Manchester, Liverpool, London, and Newcastle. We'd yell at the screen as if our voices could have some magical influence over a poor offside decision by the ref or to advise him that a foul had been committed when he was looking the other way. We are a superstitious and primitive tribe, and when the match was over we'd fade back into the city like ghosts.

Englishman in New York

I don't drink coffee, I take tea, my dear
I like my toast done on the side
And you can hear it in my accent when I talk
I'm an Englishman in New York
See me walking down Fifth Avenue
A walking cane here at my side
I take it everywhere I walk
I'm an Englishman in New York

I'm an alien, I'm a legal alien
I'm an Englishman in New York
I'm an alien, I'm a legal alien
I'm an Englishman in New York

If "manners maketh man," as someone said
Then he's the hero of the day
It takes a man to suffer ignorance and smile
Be yourself no matter what they say

I'm an alien, I'm a legal alien
I'm an Englishman in New York
I'm an alien, I'm a legal alien
I'm an Englishman in New York

Modesty, propriety can lead to notoriety
You could end up as the only one
Gentleness, sobriety are rare in this society
At night a candle's brighter than the sun

Takes more than combat gear to make a man
Takes more than a license for a gun
Confront your enemies, avoid them when you can
A gentleman will walk but never run

If "manners maketh man," as someone said
Then he's the hero of the day
It takes a man to suffer ignorance and smile
Be yourself no matter what they say

I'm an alien, I'm a legal alien
I'm an Englishman in New York
I'm an alien, I'm a legal alien
I'm an Englishman in New York

I once asked my history teacher how we were expected to learn anything from his subject when it seemed to be nothing but the monotonous exploits and sordid succession of robber barons devoid of any admirable human qualities.

I failed history.

The most palatable history of the world I ever read is only 120 pages long and part of Buckminster Fuller's book Critical Path. *The robber barons are still there, but some attempt is made to explain their pathology and why they're still around today.*

History Will Teach Us Nothing

If we seek solace in the prisons of the distant past
Security in human systems we're told will always, always last
Emotions are the sail and blind faith is the mast
Without the breath of real freedom we're getting
    nowhere fast
If God is dead and an actor plays his part
His words of fear will find their way to a place in your heart
Without the voice of reason every faith is its own curse
Without freedom from the past things can only get worse

Sooner or later just like the world first day
Sooner or later we learn to throw the past away
Sooner or later just like the world first day
Sooner or later we learn to throw the past away
Sooner or later we learn to throw the past away

Our written history is a catalog of crime
The sordid and the powerful, the architects of time
The mother of invention, the oppression of the mild
The constant fear of scarcity, aggression as its child

Sooner or later
Sooner or later
Sooner or later
Sooner or later

Convince an enemy, convince him that he's wrong
Is to win a bloodless battle where victory is long
A simple act of faith
In reason over might
To blow up his children will only prove him right
History will teach us nothing

Sooner or later just like the world first day
Sooner or later we learn to throw the past away
Sooner or later just like the world first day
Sooner or later we learn to throw the past away
Sooner or later we learn to throw the past away

History will teach us nothing
History will teach us nothing

Know your human rights
Be what you come here for
Know your human rights
Be what you come here for . . .

In 1986 I toured the world on behalf of Amnesty International, along with Bruce Springsteen, Peter Gabriel, Youssou N'Dour, and Tracy Chapman. We all became great friends on that tour, and those friendships are still firm. It was interesting for us all to share space with our peers, because normally the touring experience is pretty insular, cocooned for months on end with only your own band, your manager, your crew.

We traveled, admittedly, in a private DC-10, but as if we were an old-fashioned vaudeville revue. We had a lot of fun mixed in with the utmost seriousness of our mission to raise awareness about the continuing abuse of human rights by the world's governments.

Wherever we landed, we were introduced to former political prisoners and victims of torture and imprisonment without trial, from all over the world. These meetings had a strong effect on all of us. It's one thing to read about torture but quite another to speak to a victim and be brought a step closer to a reality that is so frighteningly pervasive.

We were all deeply affected.

I had a special affinity for the people of Chile. Thousands of people had "disappeared" there during the Pinochet years, victims of murder squads, security forces, the police, and the army. Imprisonment without trial and torture were commonplace.

The Cueca is a traditional Chilean courting dance. The Cueca Solo or the dance alone, was performed publicly by the wives, daughters, and mothers of the "disappeared." Often, they danced with photographs of loved ones pinned to their clothes. This was a powerful gesture of protest and grief, and I wrote "They Dance Alone" in response.

Pinochet is gone now and Chile is a happier place, though a few years ago, when I was playing in Santiago and invited to a meeting with some government officials, I couldn't help but feel apprehensive—until I saw the smiling faces of Los Madres de Plaza de Mayo. These were the women who had danced alone, and they had treated me like an adopted son. I'd danced with them on the stage during a previous visit, in the very stadium where their sons and husbands had been tortured and murdered.

The people in the new government gave me a medal and a citation for my efforts, and the mothers of the disappeared gave me a hug. I'd lost my own mother but had inherited many more.

They Dance Alone (*Cueca Solo*)

Why are these women here dancing on their own?
Why is there this sadness in their eyes?
Why are the soldiers here
Their faces fixed like stone?
I can't see what it is that they despise
They're dancing with the missing
They're dancing with the dead
They dance with the invisible ones
Their anguish is unsaid
They're dancing with their fathers
They're dancing with their sons
They're dancing with their husbands
They dance alone, they dance alone

It's the only form of protest they're allowed
I've seen their silent faces, they scream so loud
If they were to speak these words they'd go missing too
Another woman on the torture table, what else can they do
They're dancing with the missing
They're dancing with the dead
They dance with the invisible ones
Their anguish is unsaid
They're dancing with their fathers
They're dancing with their sons
They're dancing with their husbands
They dance alone, they dance alone

One day we'll dance on their graves
One day we'll sing our freedom
One day we'll laugh in our joy
And we'll dance
One day we'll dance on their graves
One day we'll sing our freedom
One day we'll laugh in our joy
And we'll dance

Ellas danzan con los desaparecidos
Ellas danzan con los muertos
Ellas danzan con amores invisibles
Ellas danzan con silenciosa angustia
Danzan con sus padres
Danzan con sus hijos
Danzan con sus esposos
Ellas danzan solas
Danzan solas

Hey, Mr. Pinochet
You've sown a bitter crop
It's foreign money that supports you
One day the money's going to stop
No wages for your torturers
No budget for your guns
Can you think of your own mother
Dancin' with her invisible son
They're dancing with the missing
They're dancing with the dead
They dance with the invisible ones
Their anguish is unsaid
They're dancing with their fathers
They're dancing with their sons
They're dancing with their husbands
They dance alone, they dance alone

This song seems to have lent itself to many situations throughout its life. It was originally written in 1987, on the island of Montserrat during a weeklong tropical storm. The rain just kept falling and falling. I had read a newspaper report about a young man called Ben Linder, an American engineer working in Nicaragua, who was murdered by the Contras. At the time it was becoming increasingly difficult to distinguish "Democratic Freedom Fighters" from drug-dealing gangsters, or Peace Corps workers from Marxist revolutionaries. Ben died because of this confusion.

Later, the song was informally adopted by the ecology movement as a hymn to the fragility of the planet, and by radio stations across the country as they struggled to find appropriate music to express the tragedy of the Twin Towers in New York. So many innocent lives were lost, including a friend of Trudie's, Herman Sandler.

"Fragile" had found yet another home to work its comforting solace.

Fragile

If blood will flow when flesh and steel are one
Drying in the color of the evening sun
Tomorrow's rain will wash the stains away
But something in our minds will always stay
Perhaps this final act was meant
To clinch a lifetime's argument
That nothing comes from violence and nothing ever could
For all those born beneath an angry star
Lest we forget how fragile we are

On and on the rain will fall
Like tears from a star, like tears from a star
On and on the rain will say
How fragile we are, how fragile we are

On and on the rain will fall
Like tears from a star, like tears from a star
On and on the rain will say
How fragile we are, how fragile we are
How fragile we are, how fragile we are

We'll Be Together

I see me with you and all the things you do
Keep turning round and round in my mind
Forget the weather, we should always be together
And any other thought is unkind
To have you with me I would swim the seven seas
I need you as my guide and my light
My love is a flame that burns in your name
We'll be together, we'll be together tonight

We'll be together, yeah
We'll be together, yeah
We'll be together, yeah

I see you with me and all I want to be
Is dancing here with you in my arms
Forget the weather, we should always be together
I'll always be a slave to your charms
To have you with me I would swim the seven seas
I need you as my guide in my life
My love is a flame that burns in your name
We'll be together, we'll be together tonight

We'll be together, yeah
We'll be together, yeah
We'll be together, yeah

Call me baby
You can call me anything you want
Call me baby, call me, just call me

I see you with me and baby makes three
I see me with you and all the things you do
Forget the weather, we should always be together
I need you as my guide and my light
My love is the flame that burns in your name
We'll be together, we'll be together tonight

Straight to My Heart

Well, in a hundred years from now
They will attempt to tell us how
A scientific means to bliss
Will supersede the human kiss
A subatomic chain
Will maybe galvanize the brain
A biochemic trance
Will eliminate romance

But why ever should we care
When there are arrows in the air
Formed by lovers' ancient art
That go straight to my heart

A future sugar-coated pill
Would give our lovers time to kill
I think they're working far too much
For the redundancy of touch

But what will make me yours
Are a million deadly spores
Formed by lovers' ancient art
That go straight to my heart

Come into my door
Be the light of my life
Come into my door
You'll never have to sweep the floor
Come into my door
Be the light of my life
Come into my door
Come and be my wife
I'll be true. To no one but you

If it's a future world we fear
We have tomorrow's seeds right here

For you can hold them in your hand
Or let them fall into the sand

But if our love is pure
The only thing of which we're sure
Then you can play your part
And go straight to my heart

If I should seek immunity
And love you with impunity
Then the only thing to do
Is for me to pledge myself to you

But they only dealt one card
So for me it is not hard
You're the bright star in my chart
You go straight to my heart

Come into my door
Be the light of my life
Come into my door
You'll never have to sweep the floor
Come into my door
Be the light of my life
Come into my door
Come and be my wife
I'll be true. To no one but you

Rock Steady

Saw an ad in the newspaper that caught my eye
I said to my baby, "This sounds like the ticket for you and I"
It said volunteers wanted for a very special trip
To commune with Mother Nature on a big wooden ship
We took a taxi to the river in case any places were free
There was an old guy with a beard
And every kind of creature as far as the eye could see
This old guy was the boss, he said
"I won't tell you no lie
But there's more to this journey
Than is apparent to the eye"
He said he'd heard God's message on the radio
It was going to rain forever and he'd told him to go
"I'll protect you all, don't worry, I'll be father to you all
I'll save two of every animal, no matter how small
But I'll need some assistants to look after the zoo
I can't see nobody better so you'll just have to do"
I said, "Just tell me something before it's too late and
        we're gone
I mean, just how safe is this boat we'll be on?"

"It's rock steady, rock steady
Rock steady, rock steady
Rock steady, rock steady
Rock steady, rock steady"

It rained for forty days and forty long nights
I'd never seen rain like it and it looked like our old friend
Was being proved right
We had no time to worry though, there was just too
        much to do
Between the signified monkey and the kangaroo
We had to wash all the animals, we had to feed them too
We were merely human slaves in a big floating zoo
She said, "Hey, baby, I don't mean to be flip
But it seems this old man is on some power trip"

I said, "No, no, sugar, you must be wrong
I mean, look at the size of this boat we're on
We're as safe as houses, as safe as mother's milk
He's as cool as November and as smooth as China silk
He's God's best friend, he's got a seat on the board
And life may be tough but we're sailing with the Lord."

Rock steady, rock steady
Rock steady, rock steady
Rock steady, rock steady
Rock steady, rock steady

Woke up this morning and something had changed
Like a room in my house had just been rearranged
She said, "It's stopped raining and
I know the guy's kind
But if we stay here much longer
I'm gonna lose my mind"
So we said we had a mission for his favorite dove
To see if there was any mercy from this great God above
So to find dry land, away the white bird flew
We didn't need no country, just a rock would do
When the dove came back to us, he threw down a twig
It was manna from heaven and meant we could blow this gig
"But the rock's too small," he said, "can't you see?"
I said, "It's just perfect for her, it's perfect for me"

Rock steady, rock steady
Rock steady, rock steady
Rock steady, rock steady
Rock steady, rock steady . . .

I was accosted late one night on Highgate Hill by a staggering drunk. He grabbed me by the lapels and, after tranquilizing me with his foul breath, pointed to the moon, which had swollen to its fullness, and demanded of me threateningly, "How beautiful is the moon? . . . How beautiful is the moon?" He repeated it as if he would kill me if I were to give the wrong answer.

Thinking quickly and not wishing for an early toxic death, I fixed him with my eye and declaimed, "My mistress's eyes are nothing like the sun." Shakespeare is always useful, I've found, for calming down violent drunks, if only because it gives them the impression that you're crazier than they are.

"A goodly answer . . ." he said, "a goodly answer," as he set off on a tack for Kentish Town like a listing galleon.

"Sister Moon" is a song for lunatics everywhere, for all those whose sanity is dependent on the phases of the moon.

Sister Moon

Sister Moon will be my guide
In your blue blue shadows I would hide
All good people asleep tonight
I'm all by myself in your silver light
I would gaze at your face the whole night through
I'd go out of my mind, but for you

Lying in a mother's arms
The primal root of a woman's charms
I'm a stranger to the sun
My eyes are too weak
How cold is a heart
When it's warmth that he seeks?
You watch every night, you don't care what I do
I'd go out of my mind, but for you
I'd go out of my mind, but for you

My mistress's eyes are nothing like the sun
My hunger for her explains everything I've done
To howl at the moon the whole night through
And they really don't care if I do
I'd go out of my mind, but for you

Sister Moon

This song was adapted from a melody by Hanns Eisler, a colleague of Bertolt Brecht, who, like Brecht, fled from Germany to America to escape the Nazis.

I played Mack the Knife for a while on Broadway in Brecht's Threepenny Opera, *the last play to be directed by John Dexter. John had been director of Britain's National Theatre and had also brought* Equus *and M. Butterfly to the Broadway stage. He had a cruel temper and an acid wit, but I adored him. His sarcasm reminded me so much of my father.*

We met at the first read-through of the script. As we reached my first lines, I pretended (as a joke) to be afflicted with a terrible stammer. The rest of the cast were looking at each other wide-eyed, in a kind of breathless, suppressed terror. But John gave me a long, sardonic look that could have vaporized an armored tank. If there is such a thing as a withering smile, then John possessed it.

"Very droll, Tommy!" he said.

He refused to call me Sting for the entire run. Tommy Steele was his affectionate name for me, an English rock-and-roll-singer from the '50s who dabbled in acting. Tommy achieved Broadway success in the production of Half a Sixpence *and was nominated for a Tony Award. Unlike me. So Tommy it was.*

John used to invite me 'round for tea after rehearsals, having ordered these obscenely extravagant cream cakes that he himself wasn't allowed to eat because of his diabetes. My job, it appeared, was to eat these monstrosities while John drooled visibly, in an ecstasy of epicurean voyeurism.

The Secret Marriage

No earthly church has ever blessed our union
No state has ever granted us permission
No family bond has ever made us two
No company has ever earned commission
No debt was paid, no dowry to be gained
No treaty over border, land or power

No semblance of the world outside remained
To stain the beauty of this nuptial hour

The secret marriage vow is never spoken
The secret marriage never can be broken

No flowers on the altar
No white veil in your hair
No maiden dress to alter
No Bible oath to swear

The secret marriage vow is never spoken
The secret marriage never can be broken

Conversation with a Dog

I asked my dog what he thought the best in man
He said, "The love you dispense to me twice daily
    from a can"
I said, "Why do you think my question funny?
And where would you be without my money?"
I said, "There may be some quality in us you must treasure"
"It's despair," he said, "of which your money is
    the measure"
Walk like a dog, like anybody can

I said, "What about our politics, philosophy, our history?"
He said, "If there is something admirable in these it is
    a mystery"
"But there must be something in our system, tell me
    at your leisure"
"It's despair," he said, "of which your borders are
    the measure"

Walk like a dog, talk like a man
Walk like a dog, like anybody can

I said, "What about technology, computers, nuclear fission?"
"I'm terrified of radiation, hate the television"
I said, "There must be something in our scientific treasure"
"It's despair," he said, "of which your weapons are
    the measure"

"Feed me, you can beat me. I will love you 'til I die.
But don't ask for admiration and don't ever ask me why"
I said, "Why wait till now to demonstrate displeasure?"
"It's despair," he said, "of which my silence was
    the measure"

Walk like a dog, talk like a man
Walk like a dog, like anybody can

My father died in 1989. We'd had a difficult
relationship, and his death hit me harder than I'd imagined
possible. I felt emotionally and creatively paralyzed, isolated,
and unable to mourn. I just felt numb and empty, as if
the joy had been leached out of my life.

Eventually I talked myself into going back to work, and
this somber collection of songs was the result. I became
obsessed with my hometown and its history, images of boats
and the sea, and my childhood in the shadow of
the shipyards.

THE SOUL CAGES (1991)

Ships are powerful symbols for me. As a child, I watched them being built in the flash of acetylene light. Each one had great ribs of steel, like the skeleton of a sleeping giant, and was tended by massive towering cranes, which moved with the slow deliberation of grazing dinosaurs. I could see, from the pulpit of my imagination, the nave of a mighty cathedral turned upside down, or a coffin ship welded and sealed to carry us all to the next world.

The ship would grow day by day, many times taller than the houses, blotting out the sun, and then it would be gone, never to come back.

Island of Souls

Billy was born within sight of the shipyard
First son of a riveter's son
And Billy was raised as the ship grew a shadow
Her great hull would blot out the light of the sun
And six days a week he would watch his poor father
A working man live like a slave
He'd drink every night, and he'd dream of a future
Of money he never would save
Billy would cry when he thought of the future
Soon came a day when the bottle was broken
They launched the great ship out to sea
He felt he'd been left on a desolate shore
To a future he desperately wanted to flee

What else was there for a shipbuilder's son
A new ship to be built, new work to be done
One day he dreamed of the ship in the world
It would carry his father and he
To a place they would never be found
To a place far away from this town
Mm-bay mm-bay-day mm-bay
Mm-bay mm-bay-day mm-bay

Trapped in the cage of the skeleton ship
All the workmen suspended like flies

Caught in the flare of acetylene light
A working man works 'til the industry dies

And Billy would cry when he thought of the future
Then what they call an industrial accident
Crushed those it couldn't forgive
They brought Billy's father back home in an ambulance
A brass watch, a check, maybe three weeks to live

What else was there for a riveter's son?
A new ship to be built, new work to be done
That night he dreamed of the ship in the world
It would carry his father and he
To a place they could never be found
To a place far away from this town
A Newcastle ship with no coals
They would sail to the island of souls
Mm-bay mm-bay-day mm-bay
Mm-bay mm-bay-day mm-bay

Priests, seagulls, and burials at sea.

I was honored by my hometown of Newcastle a few years ago, and in my acceptance speech I had these words to say:

The River Tyne runs through this region like a silent and constant spirit. It's a symbol of continuity, of commerce, and of creativity, a symbol that our ancestors would have recognized, a symbol that defines us as a people. We run true to our course. We exhibit a quiet and resilient strength. While we are adaptable, we are not swayed easily. We know our goals and we stick to them. I was born within sight of that river. It runs through my veins, as surely as it runs through the landscape of my dreams. It is a constant recurring theme in many of my songs: All this time the river flowed endlessly to the sea. I wrote that song about the time of the death of my father, gaining some solace in the idea that one human life may come to an end, but the river carries on, just as those of us who are left must carry on. I took this image with me and the qualities it symbolized, when I traveled south all those years ago. It was this image that sustained me when I might have faltered, gave me strength when the setbacks of life may have weakened me. It fed my dreams when I reached for the stars, and then brought me back home.

All This Time

I looked out across
The river today
I saw a city in the fog
And an old church tower
Where the seagulls play
Saw the sad shire horses
Walking home in the sodium light
Saw two priests on the ferry

October geese on a cold winter's night
And all this time
The river flowed
Endlessly
To the sea

Two priests came round
Our house tonight
One young, one old
To offer prayers for the dying
To serve the final rite
One to learn, one to teach
Which way the cold wind blows
Fussing and flapping in priestly black
Like a murder of crows

And all this time
The river flowed
Endlessly
To the sea

If I had my way
I'd take a boat from the river
And I'd bury the old man
I'd bury him at sea

Blessed are the poor
For they shall inherit the earth
One is better to be poor
Than a fat man in the eye of a needle
As these words were spoken
I swear I hear the old man laughing
What good is a used-up world
And how could it be worth having?

And all this time
The river flowed
Endlessly
To the sea

All this time
The river flowed
Father, if Jesus exists
Then how come he never lived here?
Yeah, yeah
Yeah, yeah
Yeah, yeah

Teachers told us
The Romans built this place
They built a wall and a temple on the edge of the
Empire garrison town
They lived and they died
They prayed to their gods
But the stone gods did not make a sound
And their empire crumbled
'Til all that was left
Were the stones the workmen found

And all this time the river flowed
In the falling light of a northern sun
If I had my way
I'd take a boat from the river
Men go crazy in congregations
They only get better one by one
One by one
One by one, by one
One by one

I looked out across
The river today
I saw a city in the fog
And an old church tower
Where the seagulls play
Saw the sad shire horses
Walking home in the sodium light
Two priests on the ferry
October geese on a cold winter's night

The second book of Samuel, Chapter 11.
King David falls in lust with Bathsheba, the beautiful wife of Uriah the Hittite.
King David arranges for Uriah the Hittite to be killed in battle.
The king makes love to Bathsheba.
God is not pleased.
Punishment comes in Chapter 12.

Mad About You

A stone's throw from Jerusalem
I walked a lonely mile in the moonlight
And though a million stars were shining
My heart was lost on a distant planet
That whirls around the April moon
Whirling in an arc of sadness
I'm lost without you, I'm lost without you
Though all my kingdoms turn to sand and fall into the sea
I'm mad about you, I'm mad about you
And from the dark secluded valleys
I heard the ancient songs of sadness
But every step I thought of you
Every footstep only you
Every star a grain of sand
The leavings of a dried-up ocean
Tell me, how much longer
How much longer?

They say a city in the desert lies
The vanity of an ancient king
But the city lies in broken pieces
Where the wind howls and the vultures sing
These are the works of man
This is the sum of our ambition
It would make a prison of my life
If you became another's wife

With every prison blown to dust
My enemies walk free
I'm mad about you, I'm mad about you

And I have never in my life
Felt more alone than I do now
Although I claim dominion over all I see
It means nothing to me
There are no victories in all our histories
Without love

A stone's throw from Jerusalem
I walked a lonely mile in the moonlight
And though a million stars were shining
My heart was lost on a distant planet
That whirls around the April moon
Whirling in an arc of sadness
I'm lost without you, I'm lost without you

And though you hold the keys to ruin of everything I see
With every prison blown to dust my enemies walk free
Though all my kingdoms turn to sand and fall into the sea
I'm mad about you, I'm mad about you

Jeremiah Blues (Part 1)

It was midnight, midnight at noon
Everyone talked in rhyme
Everyone saw the big clock tick-in'
Nobody knew, nobody knew the time
Elegant debutantes smiled
Everyone fought for dimes
Newspapers screamed for blood
It was the best of times
Every place around the world, it seemed the same
Can't hear the rhythm for the drums
Everybody wants to look the other way
When something wicked this way comes

Sometimes they tie a thief to the tree
Sometimes I stare, sometimes it's me

Everyone told the truth
All that we heard were lies
A pope claimed that he'd been wrong in the past
This was a big surprise
Nobody knew the time
Everyone fell in love
A cardinal's wife was jailed
The government saved a dying planet
When popular icons failed

Every place around the world it seemed the same
Can't hear the rhythm for the drums
Everybody wants to look the other way
When something wicked this way comes

Sometimes they tie a thief to the tree
Sometimes I stare, sometimes it's me
Sometimes I stare, sometimes it's me

Why Should I Cry for You?

Under the Dog Star sail
Over the reefs of moonshine
Under the skies of fall
North-northwest, the stones of Faroe
Under the Arctic fire
Over the seas of silence
Hauling on frozen ropes
For all my days remaining
Would north be true?

All colors bleed to red
Asleep on the ocean's bed
Drifting in empty seas
For all my days remaining
Would north be true?
Why should I, why should I cry for you?
Dark angels follow me
Over a godless sea
Mountains of endless falling
For all my days remaining

What would be true?
Sometimes I see your face
The stars seem to lose their place
Why must I think of you?
Why must I? Why should I?
Why should I cry for you?
Why would you want me to?
And what would it mean to say
"I loved you in my fashion"?
What would be true?
Why should I, why should I cry for you?
Why should I cry?

There are similarities between the dream state and that strange fuzzy consciousness that can overtake you when writing a song. A lot of songwriters will tell you, "Oh, that song just seemed to write itself; it was as if it was already there, waiting to be discovered."

"The Wild Wild Sea" began as a dream, as disjointed fragments recalled from a night of fitful sleep. Of course, it's rare to dream in rhyming couplets, as it's rare for a dream to have a coherent narrative, so you're forced to finish a song in the cold light of day with a pen and notebook in your hand. Nonetheless, rhyming, while being a limitation, has also an element of magic to it. It is essentially a shamanic art, and to follow its winding path is to reenter that realm that is halfway between sleep and waking, where the mysterious imperative of the unconscious can reveal itself on the page.

The Wild Wild Sea

I saw it again this evening
Black sail in a pale yellow sky
And just as before in a moment
It was gone where the gray gulls fly
If it happens again I shall worry
That only a strange ship could fly
And my sanity scans the horizon
In the light of the darkening sky

That night, as I walked in my slumber
I waded into the sea strand
And I swam with the moon and her lover
Until I lost sight of the land
I swam 'til the night became morning
Black sail in a reddening sky
Found myself on the deck of a rolling ship
So far where no gray gulls fly
All around me was silence
As if mocking my frail human hopes
And a question mark hung in the canvas

For the wind that had died in the ropes
I may have slept for an hour
I may have slept for a day
For I woke in a bed of white linen
And the sky was the color of clay

At first, just a rustle of canvas
And the gentlest breath on my face
But a galloping line of white horses
Said that soon we were in for a race
And the gentle sigh turned to a howling
And the gray sky, she angered to black
And my anxious eyes searched the horizon
With the gathering sea at my back

Did I see the shade of a sailor
On the bridge, through the wheelhouse pane
Held fast to the wheel of the rocking ship
As I squinted my eyes in the rain?
For the ship had turned into the wind
Against the storm to brace
And underneath the sailor's hat
I saw my father's face

If a prayer today is spoken
Please offer it for me
When the bridge to heaven is broken
And you're lost on the wild, wild sea
And you're lost on the wild, wild sea
And you're lost on the wild, wild sea
And you're lost on the wild, wild sea

There is an old British folktale about the souls of the dead being kept under the sea in the lobster cages of a creature who is half man, half fish. Anyone who dares try to free the souls of the dead must go under the sea himself and drink with the creature. If he drinks him under the table, the souls will go free. If, on the other hand, the creature prevails, the challenger will be imprisoned forever in the cages at the bottom of the sea. You need a strong stomach to treat with this creature.

The Soul Cages

The boy child is locked in the fisherman's yard
There's a bloodless moon where the oceans die
A shoal of night stars hang fire in the nets
And the chaos of cages where the crayfish lie
Where is the fisherman, where is the goat
Where is the keeper in his carrion coat?
Eclipse on the moon when the dark bird flies
Where is the child with his father's eyes?

He's the king of the ninth world
The twisted son of the fog bells' toll
In each and every lobster cage, a tortured human soul
These are the souls of the broken factories
The subject slaves of the broken crown
The dead accounting of old guilty promises
These are the souls of the broken town
These are the soul cages
These are the soul cages
These are the soul cages
These are the soul cages

"I have a wager," the brave child spoke
The fisherman laughed though disturbed at the joke
"You will drink what I drink
But you must equal me
And if the drink leaves me standing
A soul shall go free

"I have here a cask of most magical wine
A vintage that blessed every ship in the line
It's wrung from the blood of the sailors who died
Young white bodies adrift in the tide"

"And what's in it for me, my pretty young thing?
Why should I whistle when the caged bird sings?
If you lose a wager with the king of the sea
You'll spend the rest of forever in the cage with me"
These are the soul cages
These are the soul cages
These are the soul cages
These are the soul cages

A body lies open in the fisherman's yard like
The side of a ship where the iceberg rips
One less soul in the soul cages
One last curse on the fisherman's lips

These are the soul cages
These are the soul cages
These are the soul cages
These are the soul cages

And he dreamed of a ship on the sea
It would carry his father and he
To a place they could never be found
To a place far away from this town
A Newcastle ship with no coals
They would sail to the island of souls

When the Angels Fall

So high above the world tonight
The angels watch us sleeping
And underneath a bridge of stars
We dream in safety's keeping
But perhaps the dream is dreaming us
Soaring with the seagulls
But perhaps the dream is dreaming us
Astride the backs of eagles
When the angels fall
Shadows on the wall
In the thunder's call
Something haunts us all
When the angels fall
When the angels fall

Take your father's cross gently from the wall
The shadow still remaining
See the churches fall, in mighty arcs of sound
And all that they're containing
Yet all the ragged souls of all the ragged men
Looking for their lost homes
Shuffle to the ruins from the leveled plain
To search among the tombstones
When the angels fall
Shadows on the wall
In the thunder's call
Something haunts us all
When the angels fall
When the angels fall
When the angels fall

These are my feet
These are my hands
These are my children
And this is my demand
Bring down the angels

Cast them from my sight
I never want to see
A million suns at midnight
Your hands are empty, the streets are empty
You can't control us, you can't control us anymore
When the angels fall
When the angels fall

TEN SUMMONER'S TALES (1992)

In 1992 we moved the family out to the country,
to a run-down manor house built in the sixteenth century that
needed some care and attention. The gardens were beautiful,
and walking in them was like walking into a dream. It was
called Lake House.

I felt inspired to write, and, for the first time in years,
with a genuine spirit of happiness.

There were no grand concepts, no plan, except to have fun

telling stories in as many diverse styles and moods as I could think of. It is this carefree spirit that pervades the album and helped it to become one of my most popular records.

The title was a mischievous conceit linking my surname, Sumner, with the scurrilous character in Geoffrey Chaucer's Canterbury Tales. There was nothing more to it than that, and subtitling the first and last songs "Prologue" and "Epilogue" was just further mischief.

The album artwork does include the first picture of me with a lute, something that would become significant to me in the years to follow.

There I was, stamping around the countryside with this tune in my head, declaiming gobbledygook at the birds. I knew that I needed nine syllables for the chorus—I had the melody and the rising chords beneath—but no idea what I was going to sing.

Songwriting can be a little like fishing: There are times when you land something in the net, and other times when you get "nowt." The frustrating thing was, it sounded like a hit to me even at this early stage. There must have been a few days of this frustration. The crows began mocking me audibly, and the sheep in our top meadow started to look at me with sad concern.

"Nine syllables is all I need," I would say to myself.

"Faith, have faith. If I ever, if I ever . . . lose my faith. Two syllables to go."

A crow at rest in the high treetop gave out a bisyllabic cry in the sardonic laryngitis that is crow song.

Did he really say, "In you"?

"That's it: If I ever lose my faith in you."

I ran home, with the cawing derision of the crows in my ears while the sheep resumed their grazing.

Prologue (If I Ever Lose My Faith in You)

You could say I lost my faith in science and progress
You could say I lost my belief in the holy church
You could say I lost my sense of direction
You could say all of this and worse, but
If I ever lose my faith in you
There'd be nothing left for me to do
Some would say I was a lost man in a lost world
You could say I lost my faith in the people on TV
You could say I'd lost my belief in our politicians
They all seemed like game-show hosts to me
If I ever lose my faith in you
There'd be nothing left for me to do
I could be lost inside their lies without a trace
But every time I close my eyes, I see your face

I never saw no miracle of science
That didn't go from a blessing to a curse
I never saw no military solution
That didn't always end up as something worse
But let me say this first

If I ever lose my faith in you
If I ever lose my faith in you
There'd be nothing left for me to do
There'd be nothing left for me to do
If I ever lose my faith
If I ever lose my faith
If I ever lose my faith
If I ever lose my faith in you

One of my all-time favorite movies is The Magnificent Seven. Yul Brynner, Steve McQueen, et al., starred in the 1960 remake of Kurosawa's Seven Samurai. The plot was transposed from medieval Japan to a beleaguered Mexican village in the nineteenth century. I must have seen it at least seven times. For the purposes of the song, I conflated it with the Hollywood musical Seven Brides for Seven Brothers, which I saw but once.

7/8 time seemed the only logical choice for a time signature, as I attempted to retell both stories in my own fashion.

Love Is Stronger Than Justice

(The Munificent Seven)

This is a story of seven brothers
We had the same father but different mothers
We keep together like a family should
Roaming the country for the common good
It came to pass one fateful day
We found ourselves down Mexico way
The town, the mayor, the P.T.A.
Pleading on their knees with us all to stay
We'd only stopped for a few burritos
But they told us of the trouble with los banditos
A poor little town in need of aid
My brothers and me had never been afraid
The age of chivalry is not dead
Lonesome nights in a cowboy bed
There'd be a bride for every man
Who chased away the evil gang
Love is stronger than justice
Love is thicker than blood
Love, love, love is stronger than justice
Love is a big fat river in flood

The outcome was predictable
Our banditos were despicable

Of blood we lost a dozen liters
A small price to pay for las señoritas
The town mayor was happy, but his face was glum
The maidens numbered only one
There weren't seven brides for seven brothers
I knew I had to get rid of the others
Love is stronger than justice
Love is thicker than blood
Love, love, love is stronger than justice
Love is a big fat river in flood

Mother told me I was the clever one
The seventh son of a seventh son
It all ended so happily
I settled down with the family
I look forward to a better day
But ethical stuff never got in my way
And though there used to be brothers seven
The other six are singing in heaven
For love is stronger than justice
Love is thicker than blood
Love, love, love is stronger than justice
Love is a big fat river in flood

Love is stronger than justice
Love is thicker than blood
Love, love, love is stronger than justice
Love is a big fat river in flood
Love is a big fat river in flood

In England our house is surrounded by barley fields, and in the summer it's fascinating to watch the wind moving over the shimmering surface, like waves on an ocean of gold.

There's something inherently sexy about this sight, something primal, as if the wind were making love to the barley. Lovers have made promises here, I'm sure, their bonds strengthened by the comforting cycle of the seasons.

Fields of Gold

You'll remember me when the west wind moves
Upon the fields of barley
You'll forget the sun in his jealous sky
As we walk in fields of gold
So she took her love for to gaze awhile
Upon the fields of barley
In his arms she fell as her hair came down
Among the fields of gold
Will you stay with me, will you be my love
Among the fields of barley?
We'll forget the sun in his jealous sky
As we lie in fields of gold
See the west wind move like a lover so
Upon the fields of barley
Feel her body rise when you kiss her mouth
Among the fields of gold

I never made promises lightly
And there have been some that I've broken
But I swear in the days still left
We'll walk in fields of gold
We'll walk in fields of gold

Many years have passed since those summer days
Among the fields of barley
See the children run as the sun goes down
Among the fields of gold

You'll remember me when the west wind moves
Upon the fields of barley
You can tell the sun in his jealous sky
When we walked in fields of gold
When we walked in fields of gold
When we walked in fields of gold

The title occurred to me one day while looking out at the weather, though the song ended up as an extended metaphor for sexual frustration. I particularly like the verse about Louis XVI, and the royal astrologer is my favorite. One day he'll get a whole song to himself.

Heavy Cloud No Rain

Turned on the weatherman just after the news
I needed sweet rain to wash away my blues
He looked at the chart, but he looked in vain
Heavy cloud, but no rain
Back in time with Louis XVI
At the court of the people he was number one
He'd be the bluest blood they'd ever seen
When the king said, "Hi," to the guillotine
The royal astrologer was run out of breath
He thought that maybe the rain would postpone his death
He look in the sky, but he look in vain
Heavy cloud, but no rain

Well, the land was cracking and the river was dry
All the crops were dying when they ought to be high
So to save his farm from the banker's draft
The farmer took out a book on some old witchcraft
He made a spell and a potion on a midsummer's night
He killed a brindled calf in the pale moonlight
He prayed to the sky, but he prayed in vain
Heavy cloud, but no rain

The sun won't shine 'til the clouds are gone
The clouds won't go 'til their work is done
And every morning you'll hear me pray
"If only it would rain today"

I asked my baby if there'd be some way
She said she'd save her love for a rainy day
So I look in the sky, but I look in vain
Heavy cloud, but no rain

She's Too Good for Me

She don't like to hear me sing
She don't want no diamond ring
She don't want to drive my car
She won't let me go that far
She don't like the way I look
She don't like the things I cook
She don't like the way I play
She don't like the things I say
But oh, oh, the games we play
She's too good for me
She's too good for me
She don't like the jokes I make
She don't like the drugs I take
She don't like the friends I got
She don't like my friends a lot
She don't like the clothes I wear
She don't like the way I stare
She don't like the tales I tell
She don't like the way I smell
But oh, oh, the games we play
She's too good for me
She's too good for me

Would she prefer it if I washed myself more often than I do?
Would she prefer it if I took her to an opera or two?
I could distort myself to be the perfect man
She might prefer me as I am. Oh . . .

She don't want to meet my folks
She don't want to hear my jokes
She don't want to fix my tie
She don't want to even try

She don't like the books I read
She don't like the way I feed
She don't want to save my life
She don't want to be my wife
But oh, oh, the games we play
She's too good for me . . .

P.S. *Well, let's face it . . . she is!*

Seven Days

Seven days, was all she wrote
A kind of ultimatum note, she gave to me
She gave to me
When I thought the field had cleared
It seems another suit appeared to challenge me
Woe is me
Though I hate to make a choice
My options are decreasing mostly rapidly
Well, we'll see
I don't think she'd bluff this time
I really have to make her mine
It's plain to see, it's him or me

Monday, I could wait 'til Tuesday
If I make up my mind
Wedn'sday would be fine
Thursday's on my mind
Friday'd give me time
Saturday could wait
But Sunday'd be too late

The fact he's over six feet ten
Might instill fear in other men
But not in me
The mighty flea
Ask if I am mouse or man
The mirror squeaked, away I ran
He'll murder me in time for his tea
Does it bother me at all?
My rival is Neanderthal

It makes me think
Perhaps I need a drink
I.Q. is no problem here
We won't be playing Scrabble for
Her hand, I fear
I need that beer

Monday, I could wait 'til Tuesday
If I make up my mind
Wedn'sday would be fine
Thursday's on my mind
Friday'd give me time
Saturday could wait
But Sunday'd be too late

Seven days will quickly go
The fact remains, I love her so
Seven days
So many ways
But I can't run away
I can't run away

Monday, I could wait 'til Tuesday
If I make up my mind
Wedn'sday would be fine
Thursday's on my mind
Friday'd give me time
Saturday could wait
But Sunday'd be too late

Do I have to tell a story
Of a thousand rainy days
Since we first met?
It's a big enough umbrella
But it's always me that ends up
Getting wet. Yeah, Yeah

Saint Augustine was reputedly something of a libertine in his younger days, and the phrase Lord make me chaste . . . but not yet *is attributed to him.*

I prefer the saints in my personal hagiography to have at least some basic human flaws. Otherwise the concept of sainthood just seems too unobtainable and not particularly interesting. For the purposes of the song I morphed the saint with another character, that of the great and shameless lover Don Juan. What ensues is a torrid tale of lust, infidelity, and revenge.

Saint Augustine in Hell

If somebody up there likes me
Somebody up there cares
Deliver me from evil
Save me from these wicked snares
Not into temptation, not to cliffs of fall
On to revelation, and lesson for us all
She walked into the room
On the arm of my best friend
I knew whatever happened
Our friendship would end
Chemical reaction, desire at first sight
Mystical attraction, turned out all my lights
The minute I saw her face
The second I caught her eye
The minute I touched the flame
I knew it would never die
The minute I saw her face
The second I caught her eye
The minute I touched the flame
I knew it would never die

I don't know if it's pain
Or pleasure that I seek
My flesh was all too willing
My spirit guide was weak

I was deadly certain
His thoughts for me weren't kind
A switchblade in his pocket
Murder on his mind
Blessed St. Theresa, the whore of Babylon
Madonna and my mother all rolled into one
You've got to understand me
I'm not a piece of wood
Francis of Assisi
Could never be this good

The less I need the more I get
Make me chaste but not just yet
It's a promise or a lie
I'll repent before I die

The minute I saw her face
The second I caught her eye
The minute I touched the flame
I knew it would never die
The minute I saw her face
The second I caught her eye
The minute I touched the flame
I knew it would never die

Relax, have a cigar, make yourself at home
Hell is full of high-court judges, failed saints
We've got cardinals, archbishops, barristers
Certified accountants, music critics
They're all here. You're not alone
You're never alone, not here you're not
OK, break's over . . .

The less I need the more I get
Make me chaste but not just yet
It's a promise or a lie
I'll repent before I die

The minute I saw her face
The second I caught her eye
The minute I touched the flame
I knew it would never die
The minute I saw her face
The second I caught her eye
The minute I touched the flame
I knew it would never die

The late Michael Kamen asked me to write lyrics for an instrumental song he'd written with Eric Clapton. It was an end-title song for Lethal Weapon 3, with Mel Gibson and Danny Glover as the two intrepid L.A. cops who get themselves in and out of dangerous scrapes with lots of gunplay and car chases.

While I am not by temperament drawn to these kind of films, I was intrigued by the "brief" that the producers wanted a "buddy" song, and nothing too sappy.

I came up with the phrase It's probably me *and began to work backward from the title to create a song where two men can express their love for each other while retaining their macho credentials through the veiled reticence of the title phrase. We men are strangely contradictory creatures:* Too proud to beg, too dumb to steal.

It's Probably Me

If the night turned cold
And the stars looked down
And you hug yourself
On the cold cold ground
You wake the morning
In a stranger's coat
No one would you see
You ask yourself, "Who'd watch for me?"
My only friend, who could it be?
It's hard to say it
I hate to say it
But it's probably me

When your belly's empty
And the hunger's so real
And you're too proud to beg
And too dumb to steal
You search the city
For your only friend
No one would you see

You ask yourself, "Who could it be?"
A solitary voice to speak out and set me free
I hate to say it
I hate to say it
But it's probably me

You're not the easiest person I ever got to know
And it's hard for us both to let our feelings show
Some would say
I should let you go your way
You'll only make me cry
If there's one guy, just one guy
Who'd lay down his life for you and die
It's hard to say it
I hate to say it
But it's probably me

When the world's gone crazy, and it makes no sense
And there's only one voice that comes to your defense
And the jury's out
And your eyes search the room
And one friendly face is all you need to see
If there's one guy, just one guy
Who'd lay down his life for you and die
It's hard to say it
I hate to say it
But it's probably me

I hate to say it
I hate to say
But it's probably me
I hate to say it
I hate to say
But it's probably me
I hate to say it
I hate to say
But it's probably me

Everybody Laughed but You

Everybody laughed when I told them
I wanted you, I wanted you
Everybody grinned, they humored me
They thought that someone had spiked my tea
Everybody screamed, they told me you
Would cost the moon, we'll be there soon
Everybody laughed 'til they were blue
They didn't believe my words were true
Everybody laughed but you

It's easy to lose touch with all the friends
You like so much or liked so much
Everybody laughed, they couldn't take me seriously
Abandoned me
Sometimes I would read of things they'd done in magazines
They made the scene
Everybody left with such important things to do
But I'm not blue

Everybody left but you
Everybody left but you

Many years have passed
And some have fallen by the way, I heard them say
Everybody dreamed but those who fell
Are sleeping now, they're sleeping now
Everybody climbed like ivy to the topmost branch
It was their chance
Everybody grasped 'til they were through
It's all they thought that they could do

'Cause everybody fell
Everybody fell
Everybody fell but you

Dominic Miller, an extraordinary musician and a dear friend, has been my guitarist since 1990. One day a week, he'd come down to visit me at Lake House and we'd try out rough song ideas that either of us had had in the interim. During one of these visits, he turned up with a beautiful guitar riff. I was very taken by it, and he and I worked on shaping it into a song for the rest of the morning.

That afternoon, he asked me what I thought the song would be about. I said I didn't know, but I would take a walk and try to figure it out. I took off along the riverbank for a mile or so, through the woods and up to the sheep meadow, then headed back as the sun was dipping to the west.

When I got back, the whole song was written in my head.

Dominic now thinks that I find lyrics under a rock somewhere. . . .

He could, of course, be right.

Shape of My Heart

He deals the cards as a meditation
And those he plays never suspect
He doesn't play for the money he wins
He don't play for respect

He deals the cards to find the answer
The sacred geometry of chance
The hidden law of a probable outcome
The numbers lead a dance

I know that the spades are the swords of a soldier
I know that the clubs are weapons of war
I know that diamonds mean money for this art
But that's not the shape of my heart

He may play the jack of diamonds
He may lay the queen of spades
He may conceal a king in his hand
While the memory of it fades

I know that the spades are the swords of a soldier
I know that the clubs are weapons of war
I know that diamonds mean money for this art
But that's not the shape of my heart

And if I told you that I loved you
You'd maybe think there's something wrong
I'm not a man of too many faces
The mask I wear is one

Well, those who speak know nothin'
And find out to their cost
Like those who curse their luck in too many places
And those who fear are lost

I know that the spades are the swords of a soldier
I know that the clubs are weapons of war
I know that diamonds mean money for this art
But that's not the shape of my heart
That's not the shape, the shape of my heart
That's not the shape, the shape of my heart

Something the Boy Said

When we set out on this journey
There were no doubts in our minds
We set our eyes to the distance
We would find what we would find
We took courage from our numbers
What we sought, we did not fear
Sometimes we'd glimpse a shadow falling
Then the shadow would disappear

But our thoughts kept returning
To something the boy said as we turned to go
He said, "You'll never see our faces again
You'll be food for a carrion crow"

Every step we took today
Our thoughts would always stray
From the wind on the moor so wild
To the words of the captain's child
Something the boy said
Something the boy said
Something the boy said
Something the boy said

In the circles we made with our fires
We talked of the pale afternoon
The clouds were like dark riders
Flying on the face of the moon
We spoke our fears to the captain
And asked what his son could know
For we would never have marched so far
To be food for a crow

Every step we took today
Our thoughts would always stray
From the wind on the moor so wild
To the words of the captain's child
Something the boy said
Something the boy said

Something the boy said
Something the boy said

When I awoke this morning
The sun's eye was red as blood
The stench of burning corpses
Faces in the mud

Am I dead or am I living?
I'm too afraid to care, I'm too afraid to know
I'm too afraid to look behind me
At the feast of the crow

We spoke our fears to the captain
And asked what his son could know
For we would never have marched so far
To be food for a crow
Something the boy said . . .

Epilogue (Nothing 'Bout Me)

Lay my head on the surgeon's table
Take my fingerprints if you are able
Pick my brains, pick my pockets
Steal my eyeballs and come back for the sockets
Run every kind of test from A to Z
And you'll still know nothin' 'bout me
Run my name through your computer
Mention me in passing to your college tutor
Check my records, check my facts
Check if I paid my income tax
Pore over everything in my C.V.
But you'll still know nothin' 'bout me
You'll still know nothin' 'bout me

You don't need to read no books on my history
I'm a simple man, it's no big mystery
In the cold weather, a hand needs a glove
At times like this, a lonely man like me needs love

Search my house with a fine-tooth comb
Turn over everything 'cause I won't be home
Set up your microscope, and tell me what you see
You'll still know nothin' 'bout me
You'll still know nothin' 'bout me
You'll still know nothin' 'bout me
You'll still know zip about me

Lullaby to an Anxious Child

Hush, child
Let your mommy sleep into the night until we rise
Hush, child
Let me soothe the shining tears that gather in your eyes
Hush, child
I won't leave, I'll stay with you to cross this Bridge of Sighs
Hush, child
I can help the look of accusation in your eyes
In your eyes

The world is broken and now
All in sorrow
Wise men hang their heads

Hush, child
Let your mommy sleep into the night until we rise
Hush, child
All the strength I'll need to find, I'll find inside your eyes
In your eyes

When We Dance

If he loved you
Like I love you
I would walk away in shame
I'd move town
I'd change my name
When he watches you
When he counts to buy your soul
On your hand his golden rings
Like he owns a bird that sings

When we dance
Angels will run and hide their wings

The priest has said my soul's salvation
Is in the balance of the angels
And underneath the wheels of passion
I keep the faith in my fashion
When we dance
Angels will run and hide their wings

I'm still in love with you
I'm gonna find a place to live
Give you all I've got to give
When we dance
Angels will run and hide their wings
When we dance
Angels will run and hide their wings

If I could break down these walls
And shout my name at heaven's gate
I'd take these hands
And I'd destroy the dark machineries of fate
Cathedrals are broken
Heaven's no longer above
And hellfire's a promise away
I'd still be saying
I'm still in love

He won't love you
Like I love you
He won't care for you this way
He'll mistreat you if you stay

Come and live with me
We'll have children of our own
I would love you more than life
If you'll come and be my wife
When we dance
Angels will run and hide their wings
When we dance
Angels will run and hide their wings . . .

I'm gonna love you more than life
If you will only be my wife
I'm gonna love you more than life
If you will only be my wife
I'm gonna love you night and day
I'm gonna try in every way

I had a dream last night
I dreamed you were by my side
Walking with me, baby
My heart was filled with pride
I had a dream last night

This Cowboy Song

We rode all night across an endless desert
We had no moon to light our way
And though a million stars were slowly turning
We lacked the consciences to pray
Our horses running like a devil chase us
Their feet, they hardly touched the ground
Yes, I'm familiar with a gray wolf howling
But I'm certain I never heard that sound
Devil to pay on judgment day
Would Jesus strike me down if I should pray?
This cowboy song is all I know
To bring me back into your arms
Your distant sun, your shining light
You'll be my Dog Star shining tonight

I've been the lowest of the low on the planet
I've been a sinner all my days
When I was living with my hand on the trigger
I had no sense to change my ways
The preacher asked if I'd embrace the resurrection
To suck the poison from my life
Just like an existential cowboy villain
His words were balanced on my knife
Devil to pay, on judgment day
Would Jesus strike me down if I should pray?

This cowboy song is all I know
To bring me back into your arms
Your distant sun, your shining light
You'll be my Dog Star shining tonight

Every night
Every night
All my distances afar

This cowboy song is all I know
To bring me back into your arms
This cowboy song, this cowboy life
I'll be your Dog Star shining tonight

Dog Star . . .

The Hounds of Winter

I Hung My Head

Let Your Soul Be Your Pilot

I Was Brought to My Senses

You Still Touch Me

I'm So Happy I Can't Stop Crying

All Four Seasons

Twenty-Five to Midnight

La Belle Dame Sans Regrets

Valparaiso

Lithium Sunset

◆

My Funny Friend and Me

Until

You Will Be My Ain True Love

I Need You Like This Hole in My Head

Freak the Mighty

Black and White Army

Beneath a Desert Moon

───────────────────────────

This was the second album written and recorded in Lake House.

I was enjoying these long periods at home with the family. I'd spent so much of my life in hotel rooms and concert halls.

MERCURY FALLING (1996)

I felt that at last I was living a real life. The kids would come home from school in the afternoon and we'd all have dinner together like a normal family.

I suppose the album title suggests, among other things, that my mercurial life was beginning to find some balance, like I'd finally put down roots. I'd always believed that "settling down" was anathema to creativity, but I wanted to give it a shot. I felt it was my right.

The band loved being there too. Dominic Miller, David Sancious, and Vinnie Colaiuta were all delighted not to be stuck in some airless studio for weeks on end; I even caught Vinnie, our drummer (a certified studio animal if ever there was one), walking in the garden one morning. I'd never seen him up before noon, much less out taking the air. He of course claimed that he was but sleepwalking after the previous night's carousing.

Despite the joy of our surroundings, the album opens with this rather bleak song. Its first line, Mercury falling, *had so many reverberations for me—astrological, meteorological, astronomical, mythological, as well as the idea of finding myself in the cold, desolate landscape of old age and melancholy.*

The Hounds of Winter

Mercury falling
I rise from my bed
Collect my thoughts together
I have to hold my head
It seems that she's gone
And somehow I am pinned by
The Hounds of Winter
Howling in the wind
I walk through the day
My coat around my ears
I look for my companion
I have to dry my tears
It seems that she's gone
Leaving me too soon
I'm as dark as December
I'm as cold as the man in the moon

I still see her face
As beautiful as day
It's easy to remember
Remember my love that way
All I hear is that lonesome sound
The Hounds of Winter
They follow me down

I can't make up the fire
The way that she could
I spend all my days
In the search for dry wood

Board all the windows and close the front door
I can't believe she won't be here anymore

I still see her face
As beautiful as day
It's easy to remember
Remember my love that way
All I hear is that lonesome sound
The Hounds of Winter
They follow me down

A season for joy
A season for sorrow
Where she's gone
I will surely, surely follow
She brightened my day
She warmed the coldest night
The Hounds of Winter
They got me in their sights

I still see her face
As beautiful as day
It's easy to remember
Remember my love that way
All I hear is that lonesome sound
The Hounds of Winter
They harry me down

This song is now confirmed as a bona fide "country" song, having been covered by the late, great Johnny Cash in the final years of his life. I was so proud to hear my words and music interpreted by the "master," although he did replace the last word in the second line of verse two, *stream* with *sheen,* for some reason. Whatever, he was probably just reading a misprint, and, even so, it didn't detract one bit from the final result.

I wrote my version of the song in 9/8; the guitar riff just occurred to me that way and reminded me of the gait of a galloping horse dragging a corpse. The story of a terrible accident, guilt, and redemption materialized out of the title and out of the haunting image of the riderless horse.

I Hung My Head

Early one morning with time to kill
I borrowed Jeb's rifle and sat on the hill
I saw a lone rider crossing the plain
I drew a bead on him to practice my aim
My brother's rifle went off in my hand
A shot rang out across the land
The horse he kept running, the rider was dead
I hung my head, I hung my head

I set off running to wake from the dream
My brother's rifle went into the stream
I kept on running into the salt lands
And that's where they found me, my head in my hands
The sheriff he asked me why had I run
Then it came to me just what I had done
And all for no reason, just one piece of lead
I hung my head, I hung my head

Here in the courthouse, the whole town is there
I see the judge high up in his chair
"Explain to the courtroom what went through your mind
And we'll ask the jury what verdict they find"

I said, "I felt the power of death over life
I orphaned his children, I widowed his wife
I beg their forgiveness, I wish I was dead"
I hung my head, I hung my head

Early one morning with time to kill
I see the gallows up on the hill
And out in the distance a trick of the brain
I see a lone rider crossing the plain
He's come to fetch me to see what they done
We'll ride together 'til kingdom come
I pray for God's mercy for soon I'll be dead
I hung my head, I hung my head

Let Your Soul Be Your Pilot

When you're down and they're counting
When your secrets all found out
When your troubles take to mounting
When the map you have leads you to doubt
When there's no information
And the compass turns to nowhere that you know well
Let your soul be your pilot
Let your soul guide you
He'll guide you well
When the doctors failed to heal you
When no medicine chest can make you well
When no counsel leads to comfort
When there are no more lies they can tell
No more useless information
And the compass spins
The compass spins between heaven and hell
Let your soul be your pilot
Let your soul guide you
He'll guide you well

And your eyes turn towards the windowpane
To the lights upon the hill
The distance seems so strange to you now
And the dark room seems so still

Let your pain be my sorrow
Let your tears be my tears too
Let your courage be my model
That the north you find will be true
When there's no more useless information
And the compass turns to nowhere that you know well
Let your soul be your pilot
Let your soul guide you
Let your soul guide you
Let your soul guide you upon your way

I was becoming more and more attuned to the beauty of my surroundings, watching the seasons change, perhaps for the first time. Marking the passing of the snowdrops and crocuses of February for the daffodils of March, the hanging blossoms of April. I remember marveling at the elaborate courtship dance of the mayfly all around the copper beech.

I was not living a normal life, I'll be the first to admit, living at the Lake House. It felt more like that of a nineteenth-century aesthete than rock and roll. Easily caricatured, I know, but blissful nonetheless. My days were numinous, mystical, psychedelic, and everything seemed infused with meaning. Two birds in a sycamore tree were more than just two birds, they were an entire story.

I transposed the riverbank to the Tyne, the river of my childhood. It rhymed nicely with mine.

I Was Brought to My Senses

Alone with my thoughts this evening
I walked on the banks of Tyne
I wondered how I could win you
Or if I could make you mine
Or if I could make you mine
The wind it was so insistent
With tales of a stormy south
But when I spied two birds in a sycamore tree
There came a dryness in my mouth
Came a dryness in my mouth

For then without rhyme or reason
The two birds did rise up to fly
And where the two birds were flying
I swear I saw you and I
I swear I saw you and I

I walked out this morning
It was like a veil had been removed from before my eyes

For the first time I saw the work of heaven
In the line where the hills had been married to the sky
And all around me every blade of singing grass
Was calling out your name and that our love would
    always last
And inside every turning leaf
Is the pattern of an older tree
The shape of our future
The shape of all our history
And out of the confusion
Where the river meets the sea
Came things I'd never seen
Things I'd never seen

I was brought to my senses
I was blind but now that I can see
Every signpost in nature
Said you belong to me

I know it's true
It's written in a sky as blue
As blue as your eyes, as blue as your eyes
If nature's red in tooth and claw
Like winter's freeze and summer's thaw
The wounds she gave me
Were the wounds that would heal me
And we'd be like the moon and sun
And when our courtly dance had run
Its course across the sky
Then together we would lie
And out of the confusion
Where the river meets the sea
Something new would arrive
Something better would arrive

I was brought to my senses
I was blind but now that I can see
Every signpost in nature
Said you belong to me

You Still Touch Me

Another night finds me alone
In my dreams
You still touch me
Your picture by my telephone
In that smile
You still thrill me
Now if I sleep, I sleep here alone
In my bed tonight
You still haunt me
And if I'm falling
I'm falling like a stone
In my nightmares
You still hold me

And after all that we've been through
Now I'm wondering
If you still blame me
If only half of this was true
That you believe of me
You still shame me

Dark rain will fall until I see your face
I close my eyes
I seem to hear the raindrops saying
You won't come back
You still touch me

And when I'm sick at heart and low
In my prayers
You still heal me
When I'm so sure this isn't so
In my complacency
You still shake me

I wonder if you feel the same way as I do
And you'd come back
You still touch me

Another night finds me alone
In my bed tonight
You still haunt me
You still hold me
You still touch me

This song was another of my forays into the world of country music, and it is one of the songs I am most proud of structurally. The paradox within the title itself presents an interesting conundrum. There was cynicism there certainly, but could I turn it around?

Broken marriage was a realm I'd had more than a passing acquaintance with, and while the story is by no means autobiographical, the territory was familiar to me. The narrative also lent itself perfectly to the country genre.

The first three verses are standard fare for the "misery" song, but the middle eight, in formal song structure, demand that something else has to happen, some kind of development, or catharsis, a light at the end of the tunnel.

The character looks up at the stars one night and sees an analogue there for his situation.

He chooses a star for himself, one for his wife, two for his kids, and, most tellingly, one for the man who's run off with his wife. Something in that vision gives him hope and courage, the ability to accept that life has to move on, no matter how hard you've been kicked. And so the last verse, if not exactly joyful, is meant to evoke possibility, a glimmer of hope for the future. He has lost his cynicism, and this change of heart is illuminated by the key change—half a step—and the world keeps on turning.

Whereas the obsessive in "Every Breath You Take" is doomed forever, and trapped in the same circular key—no release for him, poor thing.

"I'm So Happy" was also ratified by the country world, this time by Toby Keith. He took the song to number two on the charts, and he and I performed it together at the Country Music Awards in Nashville. I liked Toby a lot, but we didn't discuss politics. I also got to sit in the audience with the legendary Brenda Lee. She was so sweet and asked about all my kids and how Trudie was doing. Strange to think that so many years ago I bopped with my mother to "Rockin' Around the Christmas Tree." Now here was Brenda herself, treating me like a long-lost nephew.

I'm So Happy I Can't Stop Crying

Seven weeks have passed now since she left me
She shows her face to ask me how I am
She says the kids are fine and that they miss me
Maybe I could come and babysit sometime
She says, "Are you okay? I was worried about you
Can you forgive me? I hope that you'll be happy"

I'm so happy that I can't stop crying
I'm so happy I'm laughing through my tears

I saw a friend of mine
He said, "I was worried about you
I heard she had another man,
I wondered how you felt about it?"

I'm so happy that I can't stop crying
I'm so happy I'm laughing through my tears

Saw my lawyer, Mr. Good News
He got me joint custody and legal separation

I'm so happy that I can't stop crying
I'm laughing through my tears
I'm laughing through my tears

I took a walk alone last night
I looked up at the stars
To try and find an answer in my life
I chose a star for me
I chose a star for him
I chose two stars for my kids and one star for my wife
Something made me smile
Something seemed to ease the pain
Something about the universe and how it's all connected

The park is full of Sunday fathers and melted ice cream
We try to do the best within the given time

A kid should be with his mother
Everybody knows that
What can a father do but babysit sometimes?
I saw that friend of mine, he said
"You look different somehow"
I said, "Everybody's got to leave the darkness sometime"

I'm so happy that I can't stop crying
I'm laughing through my tears
I'm laughing through my tears

I'm so happy that I can't stop crying
I'm laughing through my tears
I'm laughing through my tears

All Four Seasons

With her smile as sweet as
a warm wind in summer
She's got me flying like a bird
in a bright June sky
And then just when she thinks that
I've got her number
Brings me down to the ground
with her wintry eye
That's my baby
She can be all four seasons in one day
And when the nighttime comes
with no interference
To our warm summer love
with all its charms
But like a thoroughbred horse
she can turn on a sixpence
And I find that I'm back in
Mistress Winter's arms
That's my baby
She can be all four seasons in one day

How will I know?
How can I tell?
Which side of the bed she takes
when the day begins
She can be kind
She can be cruel
She's got me guessing like a game-show fool

She can change her mind
like she changes her sweaters
From one minute to the next
it's hard to tell
She blows hot and cold
just like stormy weather
She's my gift from the Lord

or a fiend from hell
That's my baby
She can be all four seasons in one day

Watching the weatherman's
been no good at all
Winter, spring, summer
I'm bound for a fall
There are no long-term predictions
for my baby
She can be all four seasons in one day

How will I know?
How can I tell?
Which side of the bed she takes
when the day begins
She can be kind
She can be cruel
She's got me guessing like a game-show fool

If it's a sunny day I take my umbrella
Just in case the raindrops start to fall
You could say that I'm just a cautious fellow
I don't want to be caught in a sudden squall
That's my baby
She can be all four seasons in one day
That's my baby
She can be all four seasons in one day

About thirty years ago, I left my hometown and went to seek my fortune in London. I was very lucky, because I could quite easily have been in the wrong place at the wrong time and met the wrong people, but I didn't. But this song is about the alternative. It's a song about failure.

Twenty-Five to Midnight

Train I ride, don't be slow
If your whistle can blow
Fifteen miles down the track
Tell them I'm coming back
Counting poles, counting sheep
Don't be slow, I won't weep
If your wheels on the line
Were to put me on time

Just a year to the day
Since I went upon my way
To seek my fortune and fame
Be a star, change my name
And that's it more or less
'Til this midnight express
I know I can't be late
'Cause she said she won't wait
She'll just go marry Jack
So there's no turning back
And it's twenty-five to midnight and fifteen miles of track

Band I had got a break
Just one chance we had to take
Told my girl I'd be back
Left her with my friend Jack
New York City for a spell
Things didn't turn out so well
Every dive that we played
We were lucky we got paid

Mr. Train Driver please
If your speed you increase
Every cent I have now
Will be yours, this I vow
And that's it more or less
'Til this midnight express
I know I can't be late
'Cause she said she won't wait
She'll just go marry Jack
So there's no turning back
And it's twenty-five to midnight and fifteen miles of track

We called ourselves the Latino Lovers
Hawaiian shirts and top-forty covers
I didn't think I could sink this low
When drugs and booze ate all my dough
This isn't how it was meant to be
There's no such thing as a meal that's free
If I was ever to get out alive
I have to get home on time

Train I ride, don't be slow
If your whistle can blow
Fifteen miles down the track
Tell them I'm coming back
And that's it more or less
'Til this midnight express
I know I can't be late
'Cause she said she won't wait
She'll just go marry Jack
So there's no turning back
And it's twenty-five to midnight and fifteen miles of track
And it's twenty-five to midnight and fifteen miles of track

La Belle Dame Sans Regrets

Dansons tu dis
Et moi, je suis
Mes pas sont gauches
Mes pieds tu fauches
Je crains les sots
Je cherche en vain les mots
Pour m'expliquer ta vie, alors
Tu mens, ma soeur
Tu brises mon coeur
Je pense, tu sais
Erreurs, jamais
J'écoute, tu parles
Je ne comprends pas bien
La belle dame sans regrets

Je pleure, tu ris
Je chante, tu cries
Tu semes les graines
D'un mauvais chêne
Mon ble s'envole
Tu en a ras le bol
J'attends, toujours
Mes cris sont sourds
Tu mens, ma soeur
Tu brises mon coeur
Je pense, tu sais
Erreurs, jamais
J'écoute, tu parles
Je ne comprends pas bien
La belle dame sans regrets

When I was a kid at school, geography was one of my favorite subjects, and my favorite topic was, strangely enough, South America. I was fascinated by it. The mysterious romance of the names enthralled me more than anything: Amazon, Xingu, Peru, Lima, Quito. I would look dreamily at the map, imagining creepy jungle glades and high Andean cities. Valparaiso was one of the names that captured my imagination. I imagined that it meant valley of paradise and pictured old sailing ships berthed in its peaceful harbor, resting after the terrors of Cape Horn.

Some images, even imaginary ones, stay with you.

Valparaiso

Chase the Dog Star
Over the sea
Home where my true love is waiting for me
Rope the south wind
Canvas the stars
Harness the moonlight
So she can safely go
Round the Cape Horn to Valparaiso
Red the port light
Starboard the green
How will she know of the devils I've seen
Cross in the sky, star of the sea
Under the moonlight, there she can safely go
Round the Cape Horn to Valparaiso

And every road I walked would take me down to the sea
With every broken promise in my sack
And every love would always send the ship of my heart
Over the rolling sea

If I should die
And water's my grave
She'll never know if I'm damned or I'm saved
See the ghost fly over the sea
Under the moonlight, there she can safely go
Round the Cape Horn to Valparaiso

A South American shaman told me that the human eye can't filter yellow light, so the lithium in direct sunlight goes straight to the brain. Quite how he knew that lithium is a constituent element in sunlight I didn't find out. He explained further that this was why it was good to watch the sun go down, to feel calm and at peace before nightfall and before the mercury falls again.

Lithium Sunset

Fill my eyes
O lithium sunset
And take this lonesome burden
Of worry from my mind
Take this heartache
Of obsidian darkness
And fold my darkness
Into your yellow light

I've been scattered, I've been shattered
I've been knocked out of the race
But I'll get better
I feel your light upon my face

Heal my soul
O lithium sunset
I'll ride the turning world
Into another night

I see that mercury falling
I see that mercury falling
I see that mercury falling
I see that mercury falling

I spent a year working on a Disney animated film Kingdom of the Sun *with my good friend and virtuoso pianist Dave Hartley. The same team that made the very successful* Lion King *commissioned us to write a series of songs for various characters set in the Andean kingdom of the Incas.*

The project was cursed from the beginning. The director left, the script and plot would change on a weekly basis, and I was getting more and more despondent. Then one day the studio called to tell me they had uncovered some demographic research claiming that modern children switch off mentally when characters start to sing. So they didn't want songs to be attached to characters or plots, they just wanted generic musical backgrounds. I was disappointed, to say the least, pointing out that my favorite Disney movie, The Jungle Book, *would never have been completed if such research was correct.*

Eventually the movie itself morphed into a comedy called The Emperor's New Groove *and was released in 2000. I provided an end-title song, which was nominated for an Oscar.*

My Funny Friend and Me

In the quiet time of evening
When the stars assume their patterns
And the day has made his journey
And we wondered just what happened
To the life we knew
Before the world changed
When not a thing I held was true
But you were kind to me
And you reminded me
That the world is not my playground
There are other things that matter
What is simple needs protecting
My illusions all would shatter
But you stayed in my corner
The only world I know was upside down

And now the world and me
Know you carry me

You see the patterns in the big sky
Those constellations look like you and I
Just like the patterns in the big sky
We could be lost, we could refuse to try
But we made it through
In the dark night
Who would those lucky guys turn out to be?
But that unusual blend
Of my funny friend and me

I'm not as clever as I thought I was
I'm not the boy I used to be because
You showed me something different
You showed me something pure
I always seemed so certain
But I was really never sure
But you stayed
And you called my name
When others would have walked out on a lousy game
And look who made it through
But your funny friend and me

You see the patterns in the big sky
Those constellations look like you and I
That tiny planet and the bigger guy
I don't know whether I should laugh or cry

Just like the patterns in the big sky
We'll be together 'til the end this time
Don't know the answer or the reason why
We'll stick together 'til the day we die

If I had to do this all a second time
I won't complain or make a fuss
Who would the angels send?
But that unlikely blend
Of those two funny friends
That's us

The following year I was privileged to receive another nomination for "Until," a song I wrote for the movie Kate & Leopold.

Until

If I caught the world in a bottle
And everything
Was still beneath the moon
Without your love would it shine for me?

If I was smart as Aristotle
And understood the rings around the moon
What would it all matter if you loved me?

Here in your arms
Where the world is impossibly still
With a million dreams to fulfill
And a matter of moments until
The dancing ends

Here in your arms
Where everything seems to be clear
Not a solitary thing do I fear
Except when this moment comes near
The dancing's end

If I caught the world in an hourglass
Saddled up the moon
So we could ride until
The stars grew dim
Until . . .

One day you'll meet a stranger
And all the noise is silenced in the room
You'll feel that you're close to some mystery

In the moonlight
When everything shatters

You feel as if you've known her all your life
The world's oldest lesson in history

Here in your arms
Where the world is impossibly still
With a million dreams to fulfill
And a matter of moments until
The dancing ends

Here in your arms
Where everything seems to be clear
Not a solitary thing do I fear
Except when this moment comes near
The dancing's end

If I caught the world in an hourglass
Saddled up the moon
So we would ride until
The stars grew dim
Until . . .

The time
That time stands still
Until . . .

I wrote *"You Will Be My Ain True Love" for the Civil War epic* Cold Mountain. *My intention was to write in the style of a nineteenth-century ballad, all muskets and cutlasses and flying cannonballs. It was sung by Alison Krauss, and, again, I was privileged to receive an Oscar nomination.*

You Will Be My Ain True Love

You'll walk unscathed through musket fire
No plowman's blade will cut thee down
No cutlass pull will mark thy face
And you will be my ain true love
And you will be my ain true love

And as you walk through death's dark veil
The cannon's thunder can't prevail
And those who hunt thee down will fail
And you will be my ain true love
And you will be my ain true love

Asleep inside the cannon's mouth
The captain cries, "Here comes the rout"
They'll seek to find me north and south
I've gone to find my ain true love

The field is cut and bleeds too red
The cannonballs fly round my head
The infirm'ry man may count me dead
When I've gone to find my ain true love
I've gone to find my ain true love

I went to an IMAX premiere of a terrifying film about Mount Everest. At the party afterward, the producer asked me if I would ever consider writing a song about dolphins. I said no, I would not be writing a song about a dolphin. But as the party progressed, I started thinking, and before I left I told the producer I'd had the glimmer of an idea.

I Need You Like This Hole in My Head

Lady Dolphin and her dolphin beau
Were swimming out to sea one day
All the other lady dolphins smiled
But they were smiling in that subtle dolphin way

So they pretended that they'd pay it no mind
But she was female, of the jealous kind
She couldn't stand it not to ask him why
She could see that he was flattered by the twinkle in his eye

She said, "How much do you need me?
How much do you need me?
Would you stay with me 'til this ocean floor is dry?
But if you cannot find the words that say
I'm the only one you love that way
I guess we'll have to say good-bye"

He said, "My love for you is wider than the
    wide Sargasso Sea
There ain't no bigger number I know, but
I never counted every ripple on the sea"

He said that words had never failed him yet
"But before our future course is set
I have to find a way to win you, dear
But there's two atmospheres of pressure on me here

How much do I need you?
How much do I need you?
Can't seem to find the words to make you stay
But remember all the things I've said
That I'll love you 'til the day I'm dead
'Cause I need you like this hole in my head
I need you like this hole in my head"

In 1997 I met Kipper, who turned up in my studio one day in the company of a film composer. I had been asked to provide a song for the Miramax film The Mighty, based on Rodman Philbrick's novel Freak the Mighty *about a pair of school misfits who join together to become the eponymous hero. It is my practice before starting work on a song for a film to listen to the existing score for ideas that I can integrate, so that the end product will have at least some continuity with the rest of the film. Kipper was at the time working as a programmer, and he was there to help me sift through the music cues. I liked him immediately; he had insatiable, infectious energy, an ebullient personality, and a name only marginally less silly than mine.*

The film was very good and starred Sharon Stone, but it flopped at the box office. Miramax had changed the original title to The Mighty *because they thought the word* freak *would upset their intended demographic, which I thought was wet. But it remained steadfastly the title of the song at the end of the film, of which I have remained rather proud.*

Freak the Mighty

Walking this high road
Are warriors from an olden time
A curse on this land
Oh, the days far behind us
Dragons we've slain
Rescued many maidens fair
No man ever dared break our stride
Or the brotherhood that binds us

Brothers are we
Marching on the roads of time
From this broken land
And the days that defined us
Well, all men are free
Justice is a sword we hold

Trusting in the knight's noble vow
In the brotherhood that binds us

Freak the mighty, freak the mighty

When the broken are strong
When the beaten are proud
When the twisted can stand
When the silenced can laugh
When the haunted have turned
When the tortured are sane
When the blinded still stare
When the poisoned remain
When the voiceless can sing
When the shackled can run
And this downtrodden man
Holds his face to the sun
We'll be walking high above the world
Our legend will say

Freak the mighty

In 1998 my football team, Newcastle United, reached the FA Cup final against Arsenal. As we hadn't won a major trophy since 1969, it was a big deal for me to be asked by the club to write a song for the occasion.

Anyone visiting Newcastle on any given day is always struck by how many people are wearing the black and white stripes for which the team is famous. You can witness whole families foraging zebralike on Northumberland Street.

We were very much the underdogs in '98 and the lyrics reflect that, but they also reflect our fierce local pride.

We lost the match, 2–0.

Black and White Army

Woke up early this morning and I jumped out of bed
I didn't have to wear my work clothes
I put on this shirt instead
It's a black and white jersey, it's a thing I couldn't hide
'Cos it's almost a religion and I wear it with some pride

Now the streets are all empty in this little town of mine
I was born to make this journey like the ships outside
I've got my ticket to London, and a little bit of cash
I've got this black and white jersey nice and clean
        for the match

Now tell me, why is the whole world staring?
Must be the shirt I'm wearing
Black and white army
Bringing the pride back home (we'll be)
Bringing the pride back home
Bringing the pride back home
Black and white army

It's been a long hard season, been a long hard year
And they're telling us that we're lucky

So lucky, to be here
But if we all stand together and hold our heads up high
We will raise up our voices and tell it to the sky
This time they can't deny us
This time they won't get by us

Black and white army
Bringing the pride back home (we'll be)
Bringing the pride back home
Bringing the pride back home
Black and white army

You'll never understand us if you thought that we'd give up
'Cos it's more than just a game,
And it's more than just a cup
'Cos we're marching the length of England
And I wouldn't tell no lie
I'll wear this black and white jersey 'til the day I die

Now tell me, why is the whole world staring?
Must be the shirt I'm wearing
Black and white army
Bringing the pride back home (we'll be)
Bringing the pride back home
Bringing the pride back home
Black and white army

Beneath a Desert Moon

From the mountains of the moon to the mighty delta
From the deserts of the west to the shining sea
Beneath the canopy of stars flowed the serpent river
Flowing through my father's land that he left to me
From the baker to the priest to the candle maker
From the highest to the low in my father's land
We make our offer to the sun 'fore the break of morning
Or else everything we have will just turn to sand

I have a lot to ask
I have a lot that I need to say
I have so much to do
And all I need is another day

From the soldier to the scribe to the carpet maker
All the different colored threads in a carpet loom
A woven tapestry of life is our mighty nation
This is the writing on the wall of my father's tomb

We have a lot to ask
We have a lot that we need to say
We have so much to do
And all we need is another day

Beneath the desert moon I call you
Beneath the desert moon I sing
Beneath the desert moon so lonely
I'm just a boy who would be king

With just the moon to guide us
We sometimes lose our way
If there's a light inside us
We'll follow, follow it to the brightness of the day

Every single blade of grass, every yellow flower
Every ripple on the sea or the blue blue Nile

Every leaf on every tree, every single creature
From the smallest little bird to the crocodile

We have a lot to ask
We have a lot that we need to say
We have so much to do
And all we need is another day

Beneath the desert moon I call you
Beneath the desert moon we sing
Beneath the desert moon we're waiting
Before the coming of the king

Beneath the desert moon that's sinking
We see the eastern skies on fire
This is where darkness leaves
And shining waters fall
And let the shadows run
And we'll say, "Welcome to the sun"

Brand new day . . .

From the mountains of the moon to the mighty delta
From the deserts of the west to the shining sea
Beneath the canopy of stars flowed the serpent river
Flowing through my father's land that he left to me

A Thousand Years

Desert Rose

Big Lie, Small World

After the Rain Has Fallen

Perfect Love . . . Gone Wrong

Tomorrow We'll See

Fill Her Up

Ghost Story

Brand New Day

◆

End of the Game

Song for Kenny's Dienda

All Would Envy

Before I met Kipper, *I'd been doing all my own programming. It's actually very laborious. We imagine that computers help us save time, but they just present us with more options than we can deal with. I was spending more time sequencing drum and keyboard parts than I was composing.*

Impulsively, I asked Kipper if he would come and work with me at our house in Italy. I'd seen how quickly he worked on "Freak the Mighty." The idea was that we would work together for a few days and see how things progressed. It went well—so well, in fact, that Kipper ended up staying for the next two albums, and together we became a kind of musical Freak the Mighty.

At the time that we were working on this album, there was a lot of premillennial hokum about the "end being nigh," doomsday, and Y2K. I wanted to go against all that and sing something optimistic. Optimism, I've always thought, is the best strategy. Who but the most cynical of us would want to be right about the end of the world? No, I think we make the world every day. Collectively, individually, by intention or accident, we dream our world into being. We just have to be careful what we dream.

Kipper was playing a lovely sequence of elegiac chords one morning in the studio. I soon became obsessed with trying to unearth a song from this bedrock. I locked myself away for days, appearing only briefly at dinner, before scurrying back to my rooms, hollow-eyed and largely uncommunicative. Some songs are a walk in the park, while others are more difficult quarry.

And the image of the Tower of Souls *would* come back to haunt me after the archmillennialist's *coup de théâtre* of 9/11.

A Thousand Years

A thousand years, a thousand more
A thousand times a million doors to eternity
I may have lived a thousand lives, a thousand times
An endless turning stairway climbs
To a tower of souls
If it takes another thousand years, a thousand wars
The towers rise to numberless floors in space
I could shed another million tears, a million breaths
A million names but only one truth to face

A million roads, a million fears
A million suns, ten million years of uncertainty
I could speak a million lies, a million songs
A million rights, a million wrongs in this balance of time
But if there was a single truth, a single light
A single thought, a singular touch of grace
Then following this single point, this single flame
The single haunted memory of your face
I still love you
I still want you
A thousand times the mysteries unfold themselves
Like galaxies in my head

I may be numberless, I may be innocent
I may know many things, I may be ignorant
Or I could ride with kings and conquer many lands

Or win this world at cards and let it slip my hands
I could be cannon food, destroyed a thousand times
Reborn as fortune's child to judge another's crimes
Or wear this pilgrim's cloak, or be a common thief
I've kept this single faith, I have but one belief
I still love you
I still want you
A thousand times the mysteries unfold themselves
Like galaxies in my head
On and on the mysteries unwind themselves
Eternities still unsaid
'Til you love me

I'd been spending quite a bit of time in Paris and became very excited about the Arab music scene there. Rai music had begun in the seedy clubs of colonial Algeria and, like the jazz of the New Orleans "sporting" houses before it, would rise above its questionable past and become a vibrant popular music in its own right. It drew liberally from oriental rhythms and inflections fused with western hybrids of pop, dance, and reggae. There was a palpable and contagious energy around this music in Paris at the time.

I improvised the melody over a sequence of descending chords in C minor; the images of the desert and the longing for rain seemed a logical progression, but the song lacked an authentic voice.

I'd seen Cheb Mami, one of the rising stars of the rai movement, perform earlier that year in Paris. I was enthralled by the unique quality of his voice—unsettlingly androgynous, birdlike, exotic, and technically dazzling. I got word to him, asking if he would be interested in working with me. A week or so later he turned up in our studio in Italy, diminutive (cheb means little) and dapper, in his perfectly pressed slacks. He listened intently to the work so far.

Mami does not speak English, nor did I tell him what I was singing about, but I indicated the section at the beginning of the song for which I wanted him to write Arabic lyrics and the melody they would have to match. He agreed and said he could return the following month. If he'd bothered to ask me what the song was about, I suppose I would have told him it was probably about spiritual longing or sexual longing, or maybe a bit of both, but he seemed happy enough with his task and flew back to Paris.

A few weeks later he was back in the studio vocal booth. The track began with Kipper's sequenced keyboard percolating expectantly, and then Mami started to improvise an intoxicating sliding melisma, reminiscent of the Islamic call to prayer. Instantly, it sounded authentic and galvanizing. He then sang the verse I'd commissioned in Arabic. His phrases matched the gait of the melody as perfectly as a horse and rider. Wow! It sounded like a hit to me. No more than a couple of takes sealed it. He removed the headphones and we sat together over mint tea.

I was curious about the new lyrics and asked him, "Mami, quel était le sens de tes paroles?" What were you singing about, Mami?

He mused for a while, savoring the bouquet of the freshly cut mint, and then, with a Gallic shrug: "Le grande desire."

I was a little taken aback.

Longing. I forgot to ask him whether it was sexual or spiritual.

Desert Rose

I dream of rain
I dream of gardens in the desert sand
I wake in pain
I dream of love as time runs through my hand
I dream of fire
Those dreams are tied to a horse that will never tire
And in the flames
Her shadows play in the shape of a man's desire

This desert rose
Each of her veils, a secret promise
This desert flower
No sweet perfume ever tortured me more than this

And as she turns
This way she moves in the logic of all my dreams
This fire burns
I realize that nothing's as it seems

I dream of rain
I dream of gardens in the desert sand
I wake in pain
I dream of love as time runs through my hand

I dream of rain
I lift my gaze to empty skies above
I close my eyes, this rare perfume
Is the sweet intoxication of her love

I dream of rain
I dream of gardens in the desert sand
I wake in pain
I dream of love as time runs through my hand

Sweet desert rose
Each of her veils, a secret promise
This desert flower
No sweet perfume ever tortured me more than this

Sweet desert rose
This memory of Eden haunts us all
This desert flower, this rare perfume
Is the sweet intoxication of the fall

Big Lie, Small World

I sat down and wrote this letter
Telling you that I felt better
Since you'd gone and I was free
I'm so happy
I have so little time to spare now
I'm wanted almost everywhere now
I make out like Casanova
Friends are always coming over

I signed my name as if I meant it
Sealed it with a kiss and sent it
The letter had improved my mood
Happy in my solitude

But halfway home I changed my tune
And when I saw my lonely room
The mirror caught my eye
When I sit down I cry

Big lie, small world
Big lie, small world

I had to intercept that letter
Telling you that I was better
I raced to catch the postman's van
He was leaving as I ran

I miss the bus I miss the train
I end up walking in the rain
Big dog chased me down the street
I hadn't had a bite to eat

Feeling sorry for myself
Wishing I was someone else
I walked across the city
'Cause I couldn't stand your pity

Big lie, small world
Big lie, small world

The place you live looks opulent
And obviously a higher rent
Than our cozy little room
I had this sense of doom

The landlord says you're out of town
That your new boyfriend's always around
The hour was getting late
So I sit down and wait

Here's the postman with my letter
Coming down the path, he'd better
Give that thing to me
I have to make him see

Begging doesn't do the trick
He thinks that I'm a lunatic
And then who comes upon the scene
But your new boyfriend, Mr. Clean

I hit the postman, hit your lover
Grabbed the letter, ran for cover
The police arrived in time for tea
Said they'd like to question me

I can only curse my fate
I have to face the magistrate
It hasn't been the best of days
I'd like to fly away

Big lie, small world
Big lie, small world

I have a lovely friend named Shyam Das. He's a Bhakti Yogi and for over thirty years has been a student of Sanskrit, the ancient language of the Vedic scriptures. He's from New York but speaks fluent Hindi and has been my guide and companion on many treks through India.

One year he took me on the pilgrim route from Hardwara to Gangotri, the source of the Ganges high in the Himalayas. When we couldn't find a hotel, or even a bed-and-breakfast, we would pitch our sleeping bags on the concrete floors of the pilgrim huts along the route. Some of the pilgrims had come to cleanse themselves and die in the source of their sacred river. Some were so infirm they were carried up the steep slopes on rough pallets.

One night we were near the palace of a maharaja, a friend of Shyam Das and a member of the same religious lineage. Shyam Das suggested we pay him a visit. By the time we got there it was well after midnight. The road was dark and before us was a massive medieval fortress. I was feeling somewhat reticent, if not a little afraid. The gates, however, were wide open, and behind them in a courtyard around an open fire were a group of sleeping sentries, their rifles clutched to their chests, their turbans comically askew. There was a powerful and pungent smell of sour milk in my nostrils and I was suddenly reminded of my late father, the milkman. I followed the rising coil of blue smoke from the fire toward the waiting stars. "Hello, Dad," I whispered to myself.

We took off our sandals and tiptoed past the soldiers in the flickering light, and then we mounted a long stone staircase to find the maharaja, resplendent in his sumptuous quarters.

Smiling in front of an enormous portrait of his great-grandfather, he greeted us.

"My security service," he began, with an almost imperceptible shake of the head, "is somewhat less than it should be, yes?"

After the Rain Has Fallen

The palace guards are all sleeping
Their fires burn into the night
There's a threat of rain on the dark horizon
And all that's left is a quarter moon of light
He climbs up through the darkness
No weapon but his surprise
The greatest thief in the high Sahara
Enters the room where a sleeping princess lies

All your money, your pretty necklace
This is my work on such a night
There's a storm coming over the mountain
I'll be gone long before the morning

After the rain has fallen
After the tears have washed your eyes
You find that I've taken nothing, that
Love can't replace in the blink of an eye

He was as gentle as the night wind
As no lover had been before
And the rings she wore for her bridegroom
Slipped from her fingers and fell to the floor

Take me with you, take me with you
Before my lonely life is set
I've been promised to another
To a man I've never even met

After the rain has fallen
After the tears have washed your eyes
You'll find that I've taken nothing, that
Love can't replace in the blink of an eye
After the thunder's spoken, and
After the lightning bolt's been hurled
After the dream is broken, there'll
Still be love in the world

She said, take me to another life
Take me for a pirate's wife
Take me where the wind blows
Take me where the red wine flows
Take me to the danger
Take me to the life of crime
Take me to the stars
Take me to the moon while we still have time

After the rain has fallen
After the tears have washed your eyes
You'll find that I've taken nothing, that
Love can't replace in the blink of an eye

After the thunder's spoken, and
After the lightning bolt's been hurled
After the dream is broken, there'll
Still be love in the world
Still be love in the world

Some people claim to be cats, others are birds, and I'm a dog. I don't mean this in a pejorative way. Like a dog, I'm loyal, trustworthy, honest, and fairly intelligent.

But despite all of these good points, dogs can get very, very jealous.

Perfect Love . . . Gone Wrong

I've had a question that's been preying on my mind
    for some time
I won't be wagging my tail for one good reason
It has to be a crime
This doghouse never was the place for me
Runner up and second best just ain't my pedigree
I was so happy, just the two of us
Until this alpha male
Turned up in the January sale

He won't love you
Like I love you
It won't be long now before that puppy goes astray
And what I like about this guy the most? . . .
He'd be my favorite lamppost
Devil take the hindmost

Je sais que c'est dur, mais il faut se faire au changement,
    tu vois
J'ai négligé le primordial pendant trop longtemps crois moi . . .
Je suis consciente, je vois bien que tu souffres, mais
    çà s'attenuera
Car c'est d'un homme plus d'un chien dont j'ai besoin
    pres de moi
Cesse donc de grogner, mon choix est fait c'est comme çà
N'en fait pas trop, ton attitude risque de t'éloigner de moi
Faut que tu comprennes, puisque tu dis m'aimer tant que çà
Desormais nous sommes trois, lui toi et moi

It's a shaggy kind of story
Would I tell you if I thought it was a lie?
But when the cat's away the mouse will play
I wouldn't dish around here
There's something fishy round here

I howl all night and I sleep all day
It takes more than biscuit, baby, to chase
        these blues away
I've got a long enough leash
I could almost hang myself
It's a dog's life loving you, baby
But you love someone else
Now he's moved by basket
I'd like to put him in a casket
I'll wear my best collar to his funeral

Ta mauvaise foi, j'aimerais bien que çà s'arrête
Me separer de toi, aujourd'hui çà trotte dans ma tête
Moi non, j'en peux plus, tu n'est q'un chien, c'est
        trop bête
La situation m'avait pourtant l'air d'être des pius nette
C'est clair, que je l'aime c'est un fait, ton égoïsme
        m'inquiète
Après toutes ces soirées passées seuis en tête à tête
Chaque chose a une fin, et c'est la fin de la fête
Pour toi, car bientôt il n'y aura plus que lui et moi,
        lui et moi

To have found this perfect life
And a perfect love so strong
Well, there can't be nothing worse
Than a perfect love gone wrong

You said I wasn't just your Christmas toy
I'd always be your boy
I'd be your faithful companion
And I would follow you through every thick and thin
Don't need nobody else
And we don't need him

The world of transsexual prostitutes is pretty far from my own experience, I'll have to admit. Trudie, however, my intrepid wife, did make a documentary about the subject for the BBC. She and her film followed the journey of three hopeful Brazilians from their homes in São Paolo and Rio to the night streets of Paris and Rome. Theirs was a harrowing story, for in the very act of realizing their fantasy of who they were, they put their lives in mortal danger. Proud and exotic, they live in a cruel, shadowy world where all the lines of gender, sexuality, show business, and vice are blurred to the point of nonexistence. The world would be a far duller place without them, but their story is essentially tragic.

Tomorrow We'll See

The streets are wet
The lights have yet
To shed their tawdry luster on the scene
My skirt's too short
My tights have run
These new heels are killing me

My second pack of cigarettes
It's a slow night but there's time yet
Here comes john from his other life
He may be driving to his wife
But he'll slow down, take a look
I've learned to read them just like books
And it's already half past ten
But they'll be back again

Headlights in the rainy street
I check, make sure it's not the heat
I wink, I smile, I wave my hand
He stops and seems to understand
The small transaction we must make
I tell him that my heart will break
If he's not a generous man
I step into his van

They say the first is the hardest trick
After that it's just a matter of logic
They have the money, I have the time
Being pretty's my only crime
You ask what future do I see
I say it's really up to me
I don't need forgiving
I'm just making a living

Don't judge me
You could be me in another life
In another set of circumstances
Don't judge me
One more night I'll just have to take my chances
And tomorrow we'll see

A friend of mine he wound up dead
His dress was stained the color red
No next of kin, no fixed abode
Another victim on this road
The police just carted him away
But someone took his place next day
He was home by Thanksgiving
But not with the living

Don't judge me
You could be me in another life
In another set of circumstances
Don't judge me
One more night I'll just have to take my chances

And no, it's just not in my plan
For someone to care who I am

I'm walking the streets for money
It's the business of love, "hey, honey"
C'mon, don't leave me lonely, don't leave me sad
It'll be the sweetest five minutes you ever had

Don't judge me
You could be me in another life
In another set of circumstances
Don't judge me
One more night I'll just have to take my chances
And tomorrow we'll see

Edward Hopper is such an evocative painter for me. The celebrated American realist painted "Gas" in 1940. It is one of his most famous works. Something about that lonely pump attendant beneath the Mobil sign set me thinking.

Fill Her Up

Mobil station where I stand
This old gas pump in my hand
My boss don't like me, got a face like a weasel
Oil on my hands and the smell of diesel
Here come a big shot from the city
V8 engine, she runs so pretty
"Fill her up, son, unleaded
I need a full tank a gas where I'm headed"

Up in the front seat a pretty redhead
"We're going to Vegas, we're gonna get wed"
"So fill her up, son, don't be staring
That's a real diamond she be wearing"

I'm gonna take my baby one day
I'm gonna fill her up and head west
I'm going find some money, all right

See those taillights heading west
I got no money to invest
I got no prospects, or education
I was lucky getting a job at this gas station

That old cash box on the top shelf
The boss is sleeping, I'll just help myself
Let's consider this as just a loan
I can sort it out later on the 'phone

I'm gonna pick my girl up tonight
I'm gonna fill her up and head west
I'm gonna show her all the bright lights
We're gonna say we lived 'fore we come home

And as I head through the woods on the way back
The evening sun is slanting through the pine trees real pretty
It's like I walked into a glade of heaven
And there's music playing
This money is cold in my hand
And a voice somewhere is saying
"Why would you wanna take that stolen thing
And what real happiness can bring?"

You're gonna fill her up with sadness
You're gonna fill her up with shame
You're gonna fill her up with sorrow
Before she even takes your name
You're gonna fill her up with madness
You're gonna fill her up with blame
You're gonna live with no tomorrow
You're gonna fill her up with pain
You're gonna fill her up with darkness
You're gonna fill her up with night
You gotta fill her up with Jesus
You gotta fill her up with light

You gotta fill her up with spirit
You gotta fill her up with grace
You gotta fill her up with heaven
You got the rest of life to face

You gotta fill her up the right way
You gotta fill her up with care
You gotta fill her up with babies
You gotta fill her up and swear
You're gonna love that girl forever
You're gonna fill her up with life
You're gonna be a loving husband
She's gonna be your loving wife
You gotta fill her up with gladness
You gotta fill her up with joy
You gotta fill her up with love
You gotta fill her up with love

Ghost Story

I watch the western sky
The sun is sinking
The geese are flying south
It sets me thinking
I did not miss you much
I did not suffer
What did not kill me
Just made me tougher

I feel the winter come
His icy sinews
Now in the firelight
The case continues

Another night in court
The same old trial
The same old questions asked
The same denial

The shadows closing round
Like jury members
I look for answers in
The fire's embers

Why was I missing then
That whole December?
I give my usual line
I don't remember

Another winter comes
His icy fingers creep
Into these bones of mine
These memories never sleep
And all these differences
A cloak I borrow
We kept our distances

Why should it follow that
I must have loved you?

What is a force that binds the stars?
I wore this mask to hide my scars
What is the power that moves the tide?
Never could find a place to hide

What moves the earth around the sun?
What could I do but run and run and run?
Afraid to love, afraid to fail
A mast without a sail

The moon's a fingernail
And slowly sinking
Another day begins
And now I'm thinking

That this indifference
Was my invention
When everything I did
Sought your attention

You were my compass star
You were my measure
You were a pirate's map
Of buried treasure

If this was all correct
The last thing I'd expect
The prosecution rests
It's time that I confessed
I must have loved you
I must have loved you

As a song, "Brand New Day" captured the spirit of optimism that is so important to me, and if you can think of a more hopeful manifestation of joy than Stevie Wonder's harmonica, then be my guest.

Brand New Day

How many of you people out there
Been hurt in some kind of love affair?
And how many times did you swear
That you'd never love again?
How many lonely, sleepless nights?
How many lies, how many fights?
And why would you want to
Put yourself through all of that again?
Love is pain, I hear you say
Love is a cruel and bitter way of
Paying you back for all the faith you ever had in your brain
How could it be that what you need the most
Can leave you feeling just like a ghost?
You never want to feel so sad and lost again

One day you could be looking
Through an old book in rainy weather
You see a picture of her smiling at you
When you were still together
Or you could be walking down the street
And who should you chance to meet
But that same old smile you've been thinking of all day?

Why don't we turn the clock to zero, honey
I'll sell the stock, we'll spend all the money
We're starting up a brand new day
Turn the clock all the way back
I wonder if she'll take me back
I'm thinking in a brand new way

Turn the clock to zero, sister
You'll never know how much I missed her

I'm starting up a brand new day
Turn the clock to zero, boss
The river's wide, we'll swim across
We're starting up a brand new day

It could happen to you
Just like it happened to me
There is simply no immunity
There's no guarantee
I say love is such a force if you find yourself in it
You need some time for reflection
You say, baby, wait a minute, wait a minute

Turn the clock to zero, honey
I'll sell the stock, we'll spend all the money
We're starting up a brand new day
Turn the clock to zero, mac
I'm begging her to take me back
I'm thinking in a brand new way

Turn the clock to zero, boss
The river's wide, we'll swim across
We're starting up a brand new day
Turn the clock to zero, buddy
Don't wanna be no fuddy-duddy
We're starting up a brand new day

I'm the rhythm in your tune
I'm the sun and you're the moon
I'm the bat and you're the cave
You're the beach and I'm the wave
I'm the plow and you're the land
You're the glove and I'm the hand
I'm the train and you're the station
I'm the flagpole to your nation

I'm the present to your future
You're the wound and I'm the suture
You're the magnet to my pole

I'm the devil in your soul
You're the pupil, I'm the teacher
You're the church and I'm the preacher
You're the flower, I'm the rain
You're the tunnel, I'm the train

Stand up, all you lovers in the world
Stand up, and be counted, every boy and every girl
Stand up, all you lovers in the world
We're starting up a brand new day

You're the crop to my rotation
You're the sum of my equation
I'm the answer to your question
If you follow my suggestion
We can turn this ship around
We'll go up instead of down
You're the pan and I'm the handle
You're the flame and I'm the candle
I'm the bee and you're the flower
You're the princess in the tower
I'm the mast and you're the sail
I'm the hammer, you're the nail

Stand up, all you lovers in the world
Stand up and be counted, every boy and every girl
Stand up, all you lovers in the world
We're starting up a brand new day

Seeing a wild creature as beautiful as a fox always takes my breath away. In all the complexity of the modern world, with its roads, railways, and power lines, these animals still hunt and forage and feed their young, as they've done for millennia.

A fox broke into our chicken house one night and killed every one of them. It was bloody carnage, but could I hunt it down with a pack of dogs and watch it being torn limb from limb just for being a fox? No. Such retaliation always struck me as barbaric. I built a stronger chicken house instead.

End of the Game

The fox has done running
And the beast is at bay
We'd run them in circles
By the end of the day
They chased him through brambles
They chased him through the fields
They'd chased him forever
But the fox would not yield

And some saw her shadow
On the crest of a hill
When the hounds were distracted
Away from the kill

One day we'll reach a great ocean
At the end of a pale afternoon
And we'll lay down our heads just like we were sleeping
And be towed by the drag of the moon

We ran through the forest
We ran through the streams
We ran through the heather
'Til we ran in our dreams

You were my lover
And I was your beau
We ran like the river
For what else did we know?

One day we'll reach a great ocean
At the end of a pale afternoon

The dogs are all worn out
And the horses are lame
The hunters and hunted
At the end of the game

Our love was a river
A wild mountain stream
In a tumbling fury
On the edge of a dream

They chased us through brambles
They chased us through fields
They'd chased us forever
But the heart would not yield

When the fox had done running
At the end of the day
I'm ready to answer
I'm ready to pay

And this river's still running
And time will come soon
Carried to the great ocean
By the drag of the moon

My dear friend and colleague Kenny Kirkland died in *November of 1998. Kenny had played keyboards on* The Dream of the Blue Turtles, Nothing Like the Sun, *and* The Soul Cages *and toured the world with me at least three times. He was an extraordinarily gifted musician, revered by his peers and loved by his friends for his sweet smile and his baffling modesty.*

Kenny told me that when he was a kid growing up in Brooklyn, while his friends were playing ball in the street, his mother made him practice his scales, arpeggios, and études. I wondered if he ever left the window open a little in the summer months, and if some of that music filtered down to his friends in the street, and if they realized what they were listening to.

I wrote this song to his tune "Dienda" and performed it at his memorial evening at the Beacon Theatre in New York.

Kenny's picture is on the wall behind my piano. I think about him every day.

Song for Kenny's Dienda

How like the fall
To be gone in a day
Just as the leaves had turned gold
I was drawn to a sound
That the wind carried down
From an open windowpane
And oh, how like a song
Or a sad melody
To linger long after the end
And the harmony rings
With the promise of spring
On a Brooklyn street

How like the fall to be gone in a day
Just as the trees had turned gold
I was drawn to this sound
That some fingers had found

But now the winter seems to stay too long
How like a song
Or a sad melody
To linger long after it's gone
Though the window is closed
And the questions it posed
On a Brooklyn street

How like the spring
To return in a day
When everything seems to be new
But here's someone who's hoping
The window is open
On that Brooklyn street again
And oh, how like a song
Or a sweet melody
To linger long after it's gone
Let the harmony ring
With the promise of spring
On a Brooklyn street

How like the fall
To be gone in a day
Just as the leaves had turned gold
I was drawn to a sound
That the wind carried down
From an open windowpane
And oh, how like a song
Or a sad melody
To linger long after the end
And the harmony rings
With the promise of spring
On a Brooklyn street

How like the fall to be gone in a day
Just as the trees had turned gold
I was drawn to this sound
That some fingers had found
But now the winter seems to stay too long
How like a song

Or a sad melody
To linger long after it's gone
Though the window is closed
And the questions it posed
On a Brooklyn street

How like the spring
To return in a day
When everything seems to be new
But here's someone who's hoping
The window is open
On that Brooklyn street again
And oh, how like a song
Or a sweet melody
To linger long after it's gone
Let the harmony ring
With the promise of spring
On a Brooklyn street

All Would Envy

Old enough to be her dad
But the young men were just mad, they nursed
    their grievances
And she was flattered by his charm
It wouldn't do her any harm, they all had their chances

He sent her flowers and limousines
She was treated like a queen
Anything she ever wanted
It was no problem for a man like him
And everyone expected soon
That she could ask him for the moon
If she would wear his ring

Knowing glances from his friends
In the homes at the weekends of high society
But he didn't give a damn
He never felt more like a man

And all the time the clock was ticking
And all would envy the older man and his beautiful
    young wife
Yes, all would envy

In a house upon a hill
She was there with time to kill
She lived a life she'd only dreamed
The life was never what it seemed
To all her friends that she'd ignored
She denied she was bored
She had no time for dancing, no time for dancing

But the clock upon the wall
That was ticking in the hall
Always reminded her

That life was going on as well
But she was happy and she would swear she wouldn't
    change a thing

And all would envy the older man and his beautiful
    young wife
Yes, all would envy

Now it's 5 o'clock am
She must have spent the night again with that
    old friend of hers
She loves to dance
She's missing more and more these days

But he's still stuck in his old ways
Perhaps she needs a little more romance
But the clock upon the wall is still ticking in the hall
She must be home soon, soon
Where a younger man would weep
He takes a pill and goes to sleep

Now who would envy the older man and his beautiful
    young wife
Who would envy?
Who would envy?

Inside

Send Your Love

Whenever I Say Your Name

Dead Man's Rope

Never Coming Home

Stolen Car (Take Me Dancing)

Forget About the Future

This War

The Book of My Life

Sacred Love

◆

That Sinking Feeling

This album was recorded in Italy and Paris, as the
United States and Britain were preparing to invade Iraq.
Optimism was somewhat difficult to maintain in the aftermath
of 9/11 and in the face of the messianic determination of our
leaders to seek revenge on an Iraqi regime that, while certainly
repellent enough, proved to be not guilty in this case.

Words in the mouths of politicians tend, more often than
not, to become devalued currency. Words like freedom and
truth *probably suffered the most, as we declared an all-out*
"war on terrorism," *which is of course absurd and the same as*
declaring "war on war."

As of this writing, we are still living with the results of this
absurdity. What should have been an international police action

became a "clash of civilizations," where the brazen disregard and lack of respect for cultures different from our own polarized the world into two opposing camps, "us and them." The mission of convincing others through logic and the rule of law became a lost battle for hearts and minds—a battle that may be lost for generations.

And so we need to reinvest in the words that are important to us, recalibrate their meaning, and, in the lexicon of the songwriter, there is no more important word than love itself.

Inside

Inside the doors are sealed to love
Inside my heart is sleeping
Inside the fingers of my glove
Inside the bones of my right hand
Inside it's colder than the stars
Inside the dogs are weeping
Inside the circus of the wind
Inside the clocks are filled with sand
Inside she'll never hurt me
Inside the winter's creeping
Inside the compass of the night
Inside the folding of the land

Outside the stars are turning
Outside the world's still burning

Inside my head's a box of stars I never dared to open
Inside the wounded hide their scars, inside this
        lonesome sparrow's fall
Inside the songs of our defeat, they sing of treaties broken
Inside this army's in retreat, we hide beneath
        the thunder's call

Outside the rain keeps falling
Outside the drums are calling
Outside the flood won't wait
Outside they're hammering down the gate

Love is the child of an endless war
Love is an open wound still raw
Love is a shameless banner unfurled
Love's an explosion
Love is the fire of the world
Love is a violent star
A tide of destruction

Love is an angry scar
A violation, a mutilation, capitulation,
Love is annihilation

Inside the failures of the light, the night is wrapped
    around me
Inside my eyes deny their sight, you'd never find me
    in this place
Inside we're hidden from the moonlight, we shift
    between the shadows
Inside the compass of the night, inside the memory
    of your face

Outside the walls are shaking
Inside the dogs are waking
Outside the hurricane won't wait
Inside they're howling down the gate

Love is the child of an endless war
Love is an open wound still raw
Love is a shameless banner unfurled
Love's an explosion
Love is the fire at the end of the world
Love is a violent star
A tide of destruction
Love is an angry scar
The pain of instruction
Love is a violation, a mutilation, capitulation
Love is annihilation

I climb this tower inside my head
A spiral stair above my bed
I dream the stairs don't ask me why
I throw myself into the sky

Love me like a baby, love me like an only child
Love me like an ocean, love me like a mother mild
Love me like a father, love me like a prodigal son

Love me like a sister, love me like the world has just begun
Love me like a prodigy, love me like an idiot boy
Love me like an innocent, love me like your favorite toy
Love me like a virgin, love me like a courtesan
Love me like a sinner, love me like a dying man

Annihilate me, infiltrate me, incinerate me, accelerate me,
    mutilate me, inundate me
violate me, implicate me, vindicate me, devastate me

Love me like a parasite, love me like a dying sun
Love me like a criminal, love me like a man on the run

Radiate me, subjugate me, incubate me, recreate me,
    demarcate me, educate me
punctuate me, evaluate me, conjugate me, impregnate me,
    designate me, humiliate me
segregate me, opiate me, calibrate me, replicate me

Great poetry doesn't necessarily make for great song lyrics, and vice versa, but sometimes a bit of William Blake or Shakespeare can set an idea in motion. In the same way a jazz player improvising over the chords of one song will quote fragments of other standards, sometimes as virtuosity, sometimes for humorous effect, I have often nicked pieces of our common poetic heritage and slipped them into my songs as collage—respectfully and, I hope, effectively and seamlessly.

Blake was deeply religious and a visionary, but he had no time for the churches, those dark Satanic Mills *as he called them in* Jerusalem.

The "certainties" of the major faiths on the planet are becoming increasingly contradictory, illogical, and dangerous. If there is one thing they agree on, it is that the world is heading for annihilation. So if we are to have a future, we must find it beyond scripture and, like Blake, create a personal mythology, looking for spiritual meaning in the daily fabric of our lives.

Send Your Love

Finding the world in the smallness of a grain of sand
And holding infinities in the palm of your hand
And heaven's realms in the seedlings of this tiny flower
And eternities in the space of a single hour

Send your love into the future
Send your love into the distant dawn

Inside your mind is a relay station
A mission probe into the unknowing
We send a seed to a distant future
Then we can watch the galaxies growing

This ain't no time for doubting your power
This ain't no time for hiding your care
You're climbing down from an ivory tower
You've got a stake in the world we ought to share

You see the stars are moving so slowly
But still the earth is moving so fast
Can't you see the moon is so lonely
She's still trapped in the pain of the past

This is the time of the worlds colliding
This is the time of kingdoms falling
This is the time of the worlds dividing
Time to heed your call

Send your love into the future
Send your precious love into some distant time
And fix that wounded planet with the love of your healing
Send your love
Send your love

There's no religion but sex and music
There's no religion but sound and dancing
There's no religion but line and color
There's no religion but sacred trance

There's no religion but the endless ocean
There's no religion but the moon and stars
There's no religion but time and motion
There's no religion, just tribal scars

Throw a pebble in and watch the ocean
See the ripples vanish in the distance
It's just the same with all the emotions
It's just the same in every instance

There's no religion but the joys of rhythm
There's no religion but the rites of spring
There's no religion in the path of hate
No prayer but the one I sing

Send your love into the future
Send your precious love into some distant time

And fix that wounded planet with the love of your healing
Send your love
Send your love

There's no religion but sex and music
There's no religion that's right or winning
There's no religion in the path of hatred
Ain't no prayer but the one I'm singing

Send your love
Send your love

Whenever I Say Your Name

Whenever I say your name, whenever I call to mind
    your face
Whatever bread's in my mouth, whatever the
    sweetest wine that I taste
Whenever your memory feeds my soul, whatever got
    broken becomes whole
Whenever I'm filled with doubts that we will be together

Wherever I lay me down, wherever I put my head to sleep
Whenever I hurt and cry, whenever I got to lie awake
    and weep
Whenever I kneel to pray, whenever I need to find a way
I'm calling out your name

Whenever those dark clouds hide the moon
Whenever this world has gotten so strange
I know that something's gonna change
Something's gonna change

Whenever I say your name, whenever I say your name, I'm
    already praying, I'm already praying
I'm already filled with a joy that I can't explain
Wherever I lay me down, wherever I rest my weary head
    to sleep
Whenever I hurt and cry, whenever I got to lie awake
    and weep
Whenever I'm on the floor
Whatever it was that I believed before
Whenever I say your name, whenever I say it loud, I'm
    already praying

Whenever this world has got me down, whenever I shed
    a tear
Whenever the TV makes me mad, whenever I'm paralyzed
    with fear

Whenever those dark clouds fill the sky, whenever I lose
the reason why
Whenever I'm filled with doubts that we will be together

Whenever the sun refuse to shine, whenever the skies
are pouring rain
Whatever I lost I thought was mine, whenever I close my
eyes in pain
Whenever I kneel to pray, whenever I need to find a way
I'm calling out your name

Whenever this dark begins to fall
Whenever I'm vulnerable and small
Whenever I feel like I could die
Whenever I'm holding back the tears that I cry

Whenever I say your name, whenever I call to mind
your face
I'm already praying
Whatever bread's in my mouth, whatever the sweetest
wine that I taste
Wherever I lay me down, wherever I rest my weary head
to sleep
Whenever I hurt and cry, whenever I'm forced to lie awake
and have to weep
Whenever I'm on the floor
Whatever it was that I believed before
Whenever I say your name, whenever I say it loud, I'm
already praying

Whenever I say your name
No matter how long it takes
One day we'll be together

Whenever I say your name
let there be no mistake
that day will last forever

This is another name for ayahuasca, or the vine of the soul, *the visionary plant medicine from the Amazon. Although I have taken it many times it still fills me with dread, and yet I am drawn to face the idea of my mortality in that way. It seems like an opportunity to rehearse the inevitable.*

Dead Man's Rope

A million footsteps, this left foot drags behind my right
But I keep walking, from daybreak 'til the falling night
And as days turn into weeks and years
And years turn into lifetimes
I just keep walking, like I've been walking for a
    thousand years

Walk away in emptiness, walk away in sorrow
Walk away from yesterday, walk away tomorrow

If you're walking to escape, to escape from your affliction
You'd be walking in a great circle, a circle of addiction
Did you ever wonder what you'd been carrying since the
    world was black?
You see yourself in a looking glass with a tombstone on
    your back

Walk away in emptiness, walk away in sorrow
Walk away from yesterday, walk away tomorrow
Walk away in anger, walk away in pain
Walk away from life itself, walk into the rain

All this wandering has led me to this place
Inside the well of my memory, sweet rain of forgiveness
I'm just hanging here in space

Now I'm suspended between my darkest fears and
    dearest hope
Yes, I've been walking, now I'm hanging from
    a dead man's rope

With hell below me, and heaven in the sky above
I've been walking, I've been walking away from Jesus's love

Walk away in emptiness, walk away in sorrow
Walk away from yesterday, walk away tomorrow
Walk away in anger, walk away in pain
Walk away from life itself, walk into the rain

All this wandering has led me to this place
Inside the well of my memory, sweet rain of forgiveness
I'm just hanging here in space

The shadows fall
Around my bed
When the hand of an angel
The hand of an angel is reaching down above my head

All this wandering has led me to this place
Inside the well of my memory, sweet rain of forgiveness
Now I'm walking in his grace
I'm walking in his footsteps
Walking in his footsteps
Walking in his footsteps

All the days of my life I will walk with you
All the days of my life I will talk with you
All the days of my life I will share with you
All the days of my life I will bear with you

Walk away from emptiness, walk away from sorrow
Walk away from yesterday, walk away tomorrow
Walk away from anger, walk away from pain
Walk away from anguish, walk into the rain

This song tells the story of a woman leaving her husband
early one morning while he's still sleeping. I narrate the story neutrally,
and I give them both a voice. I'm not here to take sides.

Never Coming Home

Well, it's five in the morning and the light's already broken
And the rainy streets are empty for nobody else has woken
Yet you turn towards the window as he sleeps
    beneath the covers
And you wonder what he's dreaming in his slumbers

There's a clock upon the table and it's burning up the hour
And you feel your life is shrinking like the petals of a flower
As you creep towards the closet you're so careful not
    to wake him
And you choose the cotton dress you bought last summer

There's a time of indecision between the bedroom
    and the door
But the part of you that knows that you can't take it
    anymore
There's the promise of the future in the creaking of the floor
And you're torn if you should leave him with a number

And in your imagination you're a thousand miles away
Because too many of his promises got broken on the way
So you write it in a letter all the things you couldn't say
And you tell him that you're never coming home

She starts running for the railway station, praying that
    her calculation's right
And there's a train just waiting there to get her to the city
    before night
A place to sleep, a place to stay, will get her through
    another day
She'll take a job, she'll find a friend, she'll make a life
    that's better

The passengers ignore her, just a girl with an umbrella
And there's nothing they can do for her, there's nothing
    they can tell her
There's nothing they could ever say would change the way
    she feels today
She'd live the life she'd always dreamed if he had only let her

Now in her imagination she's a million miles away
When too many of his promises got broken on the way
So she wrote it in a letter all the things she couldn't say
And she told him she was never coming home
She told him she was never coming home

I wake up in an empty bed, a road drill hammers in my head
I call her name, there's no reply, it's not like her to let me lie
It's time for work, it's time to go, but something's different,
    I don't know
I need a cup of coffee, I'll feel better

I stumble to the bathroom door, her makeup bag is on
    the floor
It really is a mess this place, it takes some time to
    shave my face
I'm not really thinking straight, she never lets me
    sleep this late
I'm almost done and then I see the letter

In his imagination she's a universe away
Too many of his promises got broken on the way
So she wrote it in a letter all the things she couldn't say
And she told him she was never coming home
She told him she was never coming home
She told him she was never coming home

I'm gonna live my life
And she told him she was never coming home
I'm gonna live my life in my own way

I liked the idea of the psychic car thief, who reads the atmosphere of any car that he steals and tells you what's been happening in it. He's cocky and rather sure of himself, as he retells the story of the company executive, his wife and kids, and the plaintive phone calls of his mistress. Again there are no judgments made by him, or by me, for that matter.

Stolen Car (Take Me Dancing)

Late at night in summer heat. Expensive car, empty street
There's a wire in my jacket. This is my trade
It only takes a moment, don't be afraid
I can hot-wire an ignition like some kind of star
I'm just a poor boy in a rich man's car
So I whisper to the engine, flick on the lights
And we drive into the night

Oh the smell of the leather always excited my imagination
And I picture myself in this different situation
I'm a company director, two kids and a wife
I get the feeling that there's more to this one's life
There's some kind of complication, he tells her he's alone
Spends the night with his lover, there's a trace of her cologne
And the words of his mistress, as she whispers them so near
Start ringing in my ear

Please take me dancing tonight, I've been all on my own
You promised one day we could, it's what you said
    on the phone
I'm just a prisoner of love always hid from the light
Take me dancing, please take me dancing tonight

I imagine his wife, she don't look nothing like a fool
She picks the kids up from some private school
She remembers what he told her, he was late and
    worked alone

But there's more than a suspicion in this lingering cologne
And the kids just won't be quiet and she runs a traffic light
And she drives into the night

Please take me dancing tonight, I've been all on my own
You promised one day we could, it's what you said
    on the phone
I'm just a prisoner of love always hid from the light
Take me dancing, please take me dancing tonight

So here am I in a stolen car at a traffic light
They go from red to green and so I just drive into the night

Please take me dancing tonight, I've been all on my own
You promised one day we could, it's what you said
    on the phone
I'm just a prisoner of love always hid from the light
Take me dancing, please take me dancing tonight

Forget About the Future

I know we got some history
We got some issues that we need to solve
But is it really such a mystery?
It's just the way that the world evolves
Let me ask your forgiveness, baby
My heart is ever full of sorrow
We got to move into the future maybe
And think about a new tomorrow

She said, you know I used to love you, baby
But you're thinking way too fast
So forget about the future
And let's get on with the past

So they called a 'nited nations summit
To negotiate for peace on earth
And it may be idealistic, baby
But I know what peace of mind is worth
Everybody aired their grievances
And they threw away the suture
They opened up all the wounds of the past
As they failed to find their way to the future

They said we'd better check the weather chart
Before we tie our colors to this mast
It's just too hard thinking about the future, baby
So let's just get on with the past

She said we'd better check the horoscope, honey
Just in case this feeling wasn't meant to last
It's just too hard thinking about the future
So let's just get on with the past

How many times you ever hear me say
I'm as flawed as any other human being?
There simply has to be a different way
And a whole new way of seeing

Are we doomed by all our history?
Is our love really beyond repair?
It's getting close to midnight, baby
And we ain't got time to spare

Just when I think I'm home and dry
And she's given up the fight
There's an unmistakable optimism
In romantic music and candlelight
There's this lingering perfume
The merest ghost of the past
She says, wait a minute, baby
You're moving way too fast
We'd better check the weather chart
Before we raise this mast
We'd best consult our horoscope
In case this feeling wasn't meant to last
Let's just forget about the future
And get on with the past

This War

You've got the mouth of a she-wolf
Inside the mask of an innocent lamb
You say your heart is all compassion
But there's just a flatline on your cardiogram

Yet you always made a profit, baby
If it was a famine or a feast

Yes, I'm the soul of indiscretion
I was cursed with x-ray vision
I could see right through all the lies you told
When you smiled for the television

And you can see the coming battle
You pray the drums will never cease
And you may win this war that's coming
But would you tolerate the peace?

Investing in munitions
And those little cotton flags
Invest in wooden caskets
In guns and body bags, guns and body bags

Your daddy was a businessman
And it always made good sense
You know the war can make you rich, my friend
In dollars, pounds and cents

In the temple that was Mammon's
You were ordained the parish priest
Yes, you may win this coming battle
But could you tolerate the peace?

Invest in deadly weapons
And those little cotton flags
Invest in wooden caskets
In guns and body bags
You're invested in oppression

Investing in corruption
Invest in every tyranny
And the whole world's destruction

I imagine there's a future
When all the earthly wars are over
You may find yourself just standing there
On the white cliffs of Dover

You may ask, what does it profit a man
To gain the whole world and suffer the loss of his soul?
Is that your body you see on the rocks below
As the tide begins to roll?

And you invested in this prison
From which you never got released
You may have won this war we're fighting
But would you tolerate the peace?

There's a war on our democracy
A war on our dissent
There's a war inside religion
And what Jesus might have meant

There's a war on Mother Nature
A war upon the seas
There's a war upon the forests
On the birds and the bees

There's a war on education
A war on information
A war between the sexes
And every nation

A war on our compassion
A war on understanding
A war on love and life itself
It's war that they're demanding

Make it easy on yourself
And don't do nothing

I like to sit in front of the fire at night and reflect. Memories always come up—thoughts, ideas, visions—and if you let them, ghosts will sit with you awhile, if you're not too afraid, that is.

The Book of My Life

Let me watch by the fire and remember my days
And it may be a trick of the firelight
But the flickering pages that trouble my sight
Is a book I'm afraid to write

It's the book of my days, it's the book of my life
And it's cut like a fruit on the blade of a knife
And it's all there to see as the section reveals
There's some sorrow in every life

If it reads like a puzzle, a wandering maze
Then I won't understand 'til the end of my days
I'm still forced to remember
Remember the words of my life

There are promises broken and promises kept
Angry words that were spoken, when I should have wept
There's a chapter of secrets, and words to confess
If I lose everything that I possess
There's a chapter on loss and a ghost who won't die
There's a chapter on love where the ink's never dry
There are sentences served in a prison I built out of lies

Though the pages are numbered
I can't see where they lead
For the end is a mystery no one can read
In the book of my life

There's a chapter on fathers, a chapter on sons
There are pages of conflicts that nobody won
And the battles you lost and your bitter defeat
There's a page where we fail to meet

There are tales of good fortune that couldn't be planned
There's a chapter on God that I don't understand
There's a promise of heaven and hell but I'm damned if I see

Though the pages are numbered
I can't see where they lead
For the end is a mystery no one can read
In the book of my life

Now the daylight's returning
And if one sentence is true
All these pages are burning
And all that's left is you

Though the pages are numbered
I can't see where they lead
For the end is a mystery no one can read
In the book of my life

I famously made an off-the-cuff comment about tantric sex one day that sped around the world like a digital virus and continues to reverberate even now, seventeen years later. The interpretation that tantra has to do with "staying power" is of course fatuous, but the idea that sex could be considered a sacred act seemed too much for a world media attuned to the minutiae of trivia. Sex is either scandalous—when, for example, politicians are caught in flagrante delicto—or it's used to sell cars and aftershave. In both cases, eroticism, the most powerful force in our human nature, is devalued to the point of worthlessness.

Sacred Love

Take off those working clothes
Put on these high-heeled shoes
Don't want no preacher on the TV, baby
Don't want to hear the news

Shut out the world behind us
Put on your long black dress
No one's ever gonna find us here
Just leave your hair in a mess
I've been searching long enough
I begged the moon and the stars above
For sacred love

I've been up, I've been down
I've been lonesome, in this godless town
You're my religion, you're my church
You're the holy grail at the end of my search
Have I been down on my knees for long enough?
I've been searching the planet to find
Sacred love

The spirit moves on the water
She takes the shape of this heavenly daughter
She's rising up like a river in flood

The word got made into flesh and blood
The sky grew dark, and the earth she shook
Just like a prophecy in the Holy Book

Thou shalt not covet, thou shalt not steal
Thou shalt not doubt that this love is real
So I got down on my knees and I prayed to the skies
When I looked up could I trust my eyes?
All the saints and angels and the stars up above
They all bowed down to the flower of creation
Every man, every woman
Every race, every nation
It all comes down to this
Sacred love

Don't need no doctor, don't need no pills
I got a cure for the country's ills
Here she comes like a river in flood
The word got made into flesh and blood
Thou shalt not steal, thou shalt not kill
But if you don't love her your best friend will

All the saints up in heaven and the stars up above
It all comes down, it all comes down
It all comes down to love

Take off your working clothes
Put on your long black dress
And your high-heeled shoes
Just leave your hair in a mess

I've been thinking 'bout religion
I've been thinking 'bout the things that we believe
I've been thinking 'bout the Bible
I've been thinking 'bout Adam and Eve
I've been thinking 'bout the garden
I've been thinking 'bout the tree of knowledge and
     the tree of life

I've been thinking 'bout forbidden fruit
I've been thinking 'bout a man and his wife

I been thinking 'bout, thinking 'bout
Sacred love, sacred love . . .

That Sinking Feeling

Have you ever had that sinking feeling
Have you faced a situation where you finally had to
    lose control
And she may have knocked your senses reeling
Now she's stolen your heart and wants to take your soul

You thought life was like an ocean liner
And nothing could be finer than to be sailing on
    the deep blue sea
But when you're sailing dangerous waters like this
There may be rocks that you miss
And then you could end up as a wreck like me
Do you remember how your sails were so high
And you were blowing the sky
Just like a galleon on the Spanish main
But you were ambushed by a twinkling eye
And you never got back to Spain
You went down and down and down
And here comes that sinking feeling again

Did you ever hear of Ulysses
The man was ever ill at ease
He was trying to get back home again
From fighting in the siege of Troy

But he was lost upon the ocean
In a circulary motion
So he couldn't find the island
Where he'd left his wife and only boy

When he heard a female voice
That didn't leave him any choice
They had to tie him to the mast
To stop him swimming ashore

He knew it couldn't be his wife
But he was begging for a knife

And then it didn't seem to matter no more
And was it really so surprising
When the waters kept on rising
It was easier surviving the war

And he'd go down and down
And here comes that sinking feeling
Once more

And when it comes to things like catching a fish
No matter how hard you wish
A woman's smarter than the average male
And even though you could have written the book
You're only bait on her hook
You always end up in the fishing pail
It's been the same way since the world began
You're only marginally smarter than Neanderthal man
All around the fishing grounds
Your proud little boats are upside down

While looking through my telescope
I spied a single periscope
I steer the ship, don't ask me how
Torpedoes off the starboard bow
It's just as if you'd struck a mountain of ice
And the *Titanic* was twice the ship
In which you find yourself afloat
And here you are in the proverbial creek
And if the fishes could speak
You got no paddle or a viable boat
And all the Democrats start jumping the ship
Electing not to sink or swim with me
So if you want to find my heart
You ought to check the bottom of the sea

Like Jonah before me
Into the depths
My heart is sinking
And here's me thinking I'm homeward bound
But my ship of love

Has run aground
To a watery grave ten fathoms down
That's when that sinking feeling
That's when that sinking feeling
That's when that sinking feeling
Comes around

Index by First Line

Photo Credits

Grateful acknowledgment is made to the following for
providing the photos used throughout the book:

ii	Kevin Mazur / WireImage
2	Fin Costello / RedFerns
24	© Jill Furmanovsky / rockarchive.com
31	© Jill Furmanovsky / rockarchive.com
38	© Barry Schultz / Sunshine / Retna Ltd.
52	Duane Michals
74	Duane Michals
89	Danny Clinch
96	Lou Salvatore
103	www.BrianArisOnline.com
116	Lou Salvatore
129	www.BrianArisOnline.com
142	© Jill Furmanovsky / rockarchive.com
153	Olaf Heine
160	Kevin Westenberg
190	© Jill Furmanovsky / rockarchive.com
226	Olaf Heine
245	From the film *Radio On* / British Film Institute
260	Fabrizio Ferri
289	Olaf Heine